DESTINATION
Atlantic Way

The Wild Atlantic Way
Ireland's Wild West Coast Road Trip

Gemma Spence and Campbell Kerr
Destination Earth Guides

32 MAGHERA BEACH

FOREWORD

After writing two books on Scotland, we decided it was time to take Destination Earth Guides further afield from our bonnie homeland, across the water to Ireland. In the summer of 2023, our hearts bursting with anticipation, we set out on an adventure along the Wild Atlantic Way, our third time visiting this incredible part of Ireland. We had fond memories of our previous trips here and having travelled far and wide around the world we have always found Ireland to be one of those places that we will return to again and again.

For the next 2 months, we drove south down the coast from Londonderry/Derry to Cork in our motorhome, Ellie the Elddis. Throughout our journey, we fell in love, yet again, with the stunning landscapes, the wild Atlantic Ocean, the hidden gems, and the charming coastal villages along the coastline. Having found a real love for this part of Ireland over the last few years, we had a desire to share the magic we had witnessed and embarked on the journey of crafting our Destination Atlantic Way guidebook. We poured our hearts into capturing the essence of this wild Atlantic coastal route through vivid imagery and evocative storytelling. With each page, we aim to ignite your imagination and inspire you to visit this extraordinary route.

As you set off on your journey along the untamed coastline, we urge you to not only enjoy at the breathtaking landscapes but also to seize the opportunities to connect with the locals that you meet along the way. Listen to their stories, indulge in their food, and get involved in the lively traditions that breathe life into the Coastal Gaeltacht. Destination Atlantic Way was created with love and passion that we have for storytelling and sharing beautiful places that we find on our travels and has been carefully created to showcase the unparalleled beauty and immersive experiences that await you. We hope it not only serves as a valuable resource for planning your own Wild Atlantic Way adventure but also as a window into the hearts and minds of the communities that call this rugged coastline home. Together, let's treasure the beauty of this incredible route and strive to preserve it for generations to come.

ABOUT THE AUTHORS

We are Gemma and Campbell, two explorers with an insatiable desire for adventure, the outdoors, alternative living, and new experiences. In 2018, we took a leap of faith and left our full-time jobs in engineering and healthcare behind to embark on an epic journey of discovery.

For the last 5 years, we have travelled the world, embracing all that it has to offer. Our travels took us to Europe, Asia, and beyond, as we sought to connect with new cultures, admire unspoiled landscapes, and immerse ourselves in the joys of alternative living. Along the way, we discovered a passion for sharing detailed travel guides and captivating stories.

Before this trip along the Wild Atlantic Way, we spent a lot of time touring our home country of Scotland, where we published two popular travel guides on Scotland that resonated with our readers. It was during this time that the idea for Destination Earth Guides was born. We realised that our true calling was to create comprehensive travel guides that not only showcased the beauty of each destination but also provided practical tips and insider information to help fellow travellers make the most of their adventures.

In 2022, inspired by our love for Ireland and its stunning coastline, we packed up our van and set out on a journey to explore every corner of the Wild Atlantic Way, later returning to complete the route in 2023. Our goal was not only to immerse ourselves in the breathtaking scenery and vibrant culture but also to create a guidebook that would truly capture the essence of this extraordinary region.

Destination Earth Guides presents this comprehensive guidebook that combines our passion for adventure, detailed travel guides, and the beauty of the Wild Atlantic Way. Within these pages, you'll find in-depth information, insider tips, and captivating stories to accompany you on your own remarkable journey along this stunning coastline.

Join us as we share our insights, discoveries, and unwavering enthusiasm for the Wild Atlantic Way. Let this guidebook be your trusted companion as you navigate the beautiful sights, charming communities, and unique experiences that await you. We hope that through our passion, you will be inspired to embark on your own unforgettable adventure, and to cherish the wonders of this remarkable world we call home.

Welcome to the Wild Atlantic Way!

Instagram - @highlands2hammocks
Youtube - Highlands2hammocks

CONTENTS

Introduction	3
What to Expect from the WAW	5
The Wild Side of the WAW	15
Best of the Wild Atlantic Way	36

Northern Headlands and the Surf Coast
Inishowen Peninsula	50
Fanad Head	70
Sliabh Liag Coast	88
Donegal Bay and Sligo	100
Erris	114

Bay Coast & Cliff Coast
Achill Island and Clew Bay	128
Killary Harbour	144
Connemara	160
Burren and West Clare	172
The Shannon Estuary	186

Southern Peninsulas & Haven Coast
Dingle Peninsula	198
Ring of Kerry	216
Beara and Sheep's Head	234
West Cork	252

Planning Your Route
7-Day Itinerary	273
14-Day Itinerary	276
One month Itinerary	279

72 CLIFDEN CASTLE

SUMMARY OF THE Wild Atlantic Way

Scan the barcode here for access to the Destination Atlantic Way map, showing all sights listed in this book

SCAN ME

INTRODUCTION

The Wild Atlantic Way is a spectacular 2,500-km route that hugs the rugged western coastline of Ireland, offering breathtaking scenery, pristine beaches, and a wealth of unique experiences found nowhere else in the world.

The Wild Atlantic Way has been in existence for centuries, but it was not until the Irish government officially launched this epic road trip in 2014 that it became one of the world's most popular tourist destinations. This designated route provides a significant boost to the rural areas in the western region by attracting more visitors, creating thousands of jobs, and revitalising the local economy.

In this guidebook, we share with you our extensive knowledge of this magnificent coastal route, including the most beautiful sights, the best places to eat and drink, and many other tips to make your journey along the Wild Atlantic Way as comfortable and memorable as possible. Whether you are a seasoned traveller or a first-time visitor to Ireland, our guidebook provides a comprehensive resource for you to explore everything this breathtaking route has to offer.

Our aim is to encourage you to embrace the local culture, connect with the people, and immerse yourself in the sheer beauty of the Wild Atlantic Way. Be it a road trip, hiking, cycling, or surfing, this guidebook offers practical information and insider tips to help you make the most of your journey.

Whether you're reading this guidebook as you plan your adventure along the Wild Atlantic Way or have already hit the road, we invite you to sit back, relax, and enjoy the ride. From stunning landscapes to incredible local experiences, the Wild Atlantic Way has something for everyone. Let us be your guide, and let this magnificent coastal route capture your hearts, as it has captured ours.

107 DUNQUIN

What is the Wild Atlantic Way?

The Wild Atlantic Way is a breathtaking coastal drive that stretches for over 2,500 kilometres (1,550 miles) along the western seaboard of Ireland. It offers the opportunity to explore some of the most beautiful and unspoiled landscapes in the country, from rugged cliffs and golden beaches to rolling green hills and charming villages. Along the way, you'll have the chance to discover a wide range of experiences, from world-class surf breaks and breathtaking coastal drives to charming towns and villages.

One of the best things about the Wild Atlantic Way is the diverse range of experiences it offers. Whether you're interested in outdoor adventure, history and culture, or food and drink, there's something for everyone along the route. You can spend your days hiking, cycling, or surfing, and your evenings exploring the local food and drink scene or soaking up the local culture.

The Wild Atlantic Way is also a great way to discover some of the lesser-known parts of Ireland, as it takes you off the beaten path and into some of the most remote and unspoiled parts of the country. Along the way, you'll have the opportunity to meet local people and learn about the history and culture of the region.

Overall, the Wild Atlantic Way is a must-see destination for anyone interested in exploring the beauty and culture of Ireland. With its stunning landscapes, diverse range of experiences, and friendly local people, it is a journey that you will never forget.

110 SLEA HEAD

History of the Wild Atlantic Way

Created in 2014 by the Irish government as a way to boost tourism and highlight the unique beauty and culture of the region, the WAW begins in County Cork in the south and takes you north through a variety of landscapes up to the north.

The idea for the Wild Atlantic Way was first proposed in the late 2000s, as a way to capitalise on the growing interest in Ireland's western coast. The route was officially launched in 2014, and since then it has become one of the most popular tourist attractions in the country, attracting millions of visitors each and every year from all across the world.

One of the main reasons for the success of the Wild Atlantic Way is the wide range of experiences it has to offer. From adventure activities and wildlife watching to history, culture, and food and drink, there's something for everyone along the route. The journey also takes you off the beaten path and into some of the most remote and

unspoilt parts of the country, giving you the opportunity to discover the hidden gems and unexpected delights of the region.

One of the highlights of the Wild Atlantic Way is the chance to meet local people and learn about their way of life. The route takes you through a variety of communities, each with its own unique character and traditions. You'll have the opportunity to visit local farms and producers, sample traditional foods and drinks, and learn about the history and culture of the region.

The Wild Atlantic Way is a journey through the culture and history of the western coast of Ireland. From music and dance to literature and art, there's something for everyone along the route. Whether you're interested in outdoor adventure, history and culture, or food and drink, you'll find plenty of opportunities to explore and discover the unique character and traditions of the region.

Atlantic puffins - Aran Islands, the Blasket Islands, and the Skellig Islands.
Dolphins - West Cork, the Dingle Peninsula, Shannon Estuary, and Galway Bay
Whales - Clare Coast, the Aran Islands, Donegal Coast, Dingle Peninsula
Seals - Cliffs of Moher, the Beara Peninsula, and the Inishkea Islands.
Red & Roe Deer - Torc, Cores, Mangerton Mountains, Killarney National Park
Pine martens - Connemara, Killarney, and Glenveagh National Parks

Wildlife on the Wild Atlantic Way

The west coast of Ireland is home to a diverse range of wildlife, from seabirds and marine animals to land-based species. One of the most iconic and beloved animals of the region is the Atlantic puffin, which can be found in large numbers along the coast between May and June. These charming birds are known for their distinctive black and white plumage and bright orange beaks, and they can often be seen nesting on cliffs and islands along the coast. Other seabirds that can be found along the west coast of Ireland include gulls, terns, and guillemots.

The west coast of Ireland is also home to a wide range of marine animals, including dolphins, whales, and seals. Dolphin-watching tours are a popular activity along the coast, allowing visitors to get up close and personal with these intelligent and playful creatures. Whales can also be spotted off the coast throughout the year, with species such as humpbacks and minke whales commonly seen in the area. Seals are another common sight along the west coast, and they can often be seen basking on rocks or swimming in the shallow waters.

In addition to seabirds and marine animals, the west coast of Ireland is home to a variety of land-based species, including deer and badgers. We highly recommend bring binoculars and a camera with a good zoom for your road trip.

Popularity of the Wild Atlantic Way

According to the Irish Tourist Industry Confederation (ITIC), the Wild Atlantic Way was the most popular attraction in Ireland in 2019, with over 2.6 million visitors. This represents an increase of 9% compared to the previous year, and the trend is expected to continue in the coming years. In addition to attracting tourists from Ireland and the UK, the Wild Atlantic Way is also a popular destination for visitors from the US, Germany, and other European countries.

One of the main reasons for the popularity of the Wild Atlantic Way is the diverse range of experiences it offers. From outdoor adventure and wildlife watching to history, culture, and food and drink, there's something for everyone along the route. The route also takes you off the beaten path and into some of the most remote and unspoiled parts of the country, giving you the opportunity to discover the hidden gems and unexpected delights of the region.

In terms of the overall impact on Ireland, the success of the Wild Atlantic Way has been largely positive. However, it's worth noting that any increase in tourism can also have some negative impacts, such as overcrowding and pressure on local resources. It's important that tourism is managed responsibly to ensure that it continues to have a positive impact on the country and its communities.

One of the main reasons we have written this guide is to encourage visitors to spread out and slow down whilst enjoying the beauty that Ireland has to offer. We highlight, not only the most popular sights around the country, but also the lesser known gems that can only be found by straying from the herd and embracing the desire to explore.

29 CARRICKFIN BEACH

Alternative Road Trips to the Wild Atlantic Way

In addition to the Wild Atlantic Way, the Ring of Kerry, and the Sliabh Liag Coastal Drive, here are some of the other road trips in Ireland that showcase the country's beauty, culture, and history:

The Causeway Coastal Route: This road trip takes you along the stunning northern coast of Northern Ireland, offering breathtaking views of the Atlantic Ocean and iconic sites such as the Giant's Causeway, Carrick-a-Rede Rope Bridge, and the scenic Glens of Antrim.

Boyne Valley Scenic Loop: Located in County Meath, this road trip explores the ancient history of Ireland. You can visit the ancient passage tombs of Newgrange and Knowth, the Hill of Tara, and the impressive Trim Castle, among other historic sites.

These road trips offer unique experiences and allow you to immerse yourself in the stunning scenery, history, and culture of Ireland. They are all worth exploring alongside or as alternatives to the more famous routes.

110 SLEA HEAD

What to Expect from the Wild Atlantic Way

The WAW offers an unparalleled experience. As the coastal road meanders from north to south along Ireland's western coast, it unveils awe-inspiring beaches and towering cliffs, showcasing the breathtaking scenery that is truly unique to Ireland. The landscape transitions seamlessly from golden sands and crystal-clear waters to majestic mountains and deep, mystical loughs.

Driving in Ireland

Embarking on a drive through Ireland's remote regions can be an exceptional experience, granting access to some of the country's most captivating and lesser-known landscapes. However, it is crucial to bear in mind certain aspects to guarantee a safe and pleasurable journey.

Firstly, acquaint yourself with Irish roads and driving regulations. Remote roads can be narrow, winding, and poorly maintained, so it is vital to drive cautiously and anticipate unforeseen turns. Investing in a dependable GPS or map is also recommended, as cell phone service may be unreliable in remote areas.

Additionally, prepare for unpredictable weather, as Ireland's climate can be quite fickle. Ensure you have warm clothing, ample water, and snacks in case of sudden delays. It is also wise to inform someone of your travel plans and check-in regularly to confirm your safety.

Skilled drivers are preferred for navigating the Wild Atlantic Way, especially when operating larger vehicles like campervans, as many roads are single track, narrow, and winding. While cruising these serpentine roads, be prepared for the possibility of encountering sheep or deer.

In Ireland, driving is on the left side, which applies to single-track roads as well. This can be confusing, so local authorities advise wearing a band or bracelet on your left wrist to remind you of the correct side.

Passing places are designated for allowing traffic to overtake on single-track roads. Remember that these are not parking spaces. When driving on these roads, maintain a "passing place" distance from cars in front to prevent traffic jams and pull over to let oncoming vehicles pass.

The main ports to arrive into Ireland by car are at Rosslare and Dublin, as well as Belfast in Northern Ireland. From these ports you can head west to begin your journey along the western coastline. Despite being in the EU, Ireland is not a Schengen country. This means that, as a UK citizen, there is no 90 day limit and you will not require a passport to arrive from the UK. Arriving from Europe or elsewhere in the world, you will still require a valid passport as you would when arriving into the UK.

As for pets, travelling to Ireland requires the same paperwork as travelling to any other EU member state. This includes an official recognised EU pet passport with vetenary endorsements certifying compliance with tests, treatments, and vaccinations.

Driving in remote Ireland may be adventurous, but with the proper precautions and preparations, it can be an unforgettable and fulfilling experience. From striking coastlines to verdant hills and quaint villages, there is so much to discover. Drive safely and responsibly to ensure an extraordinary trip.

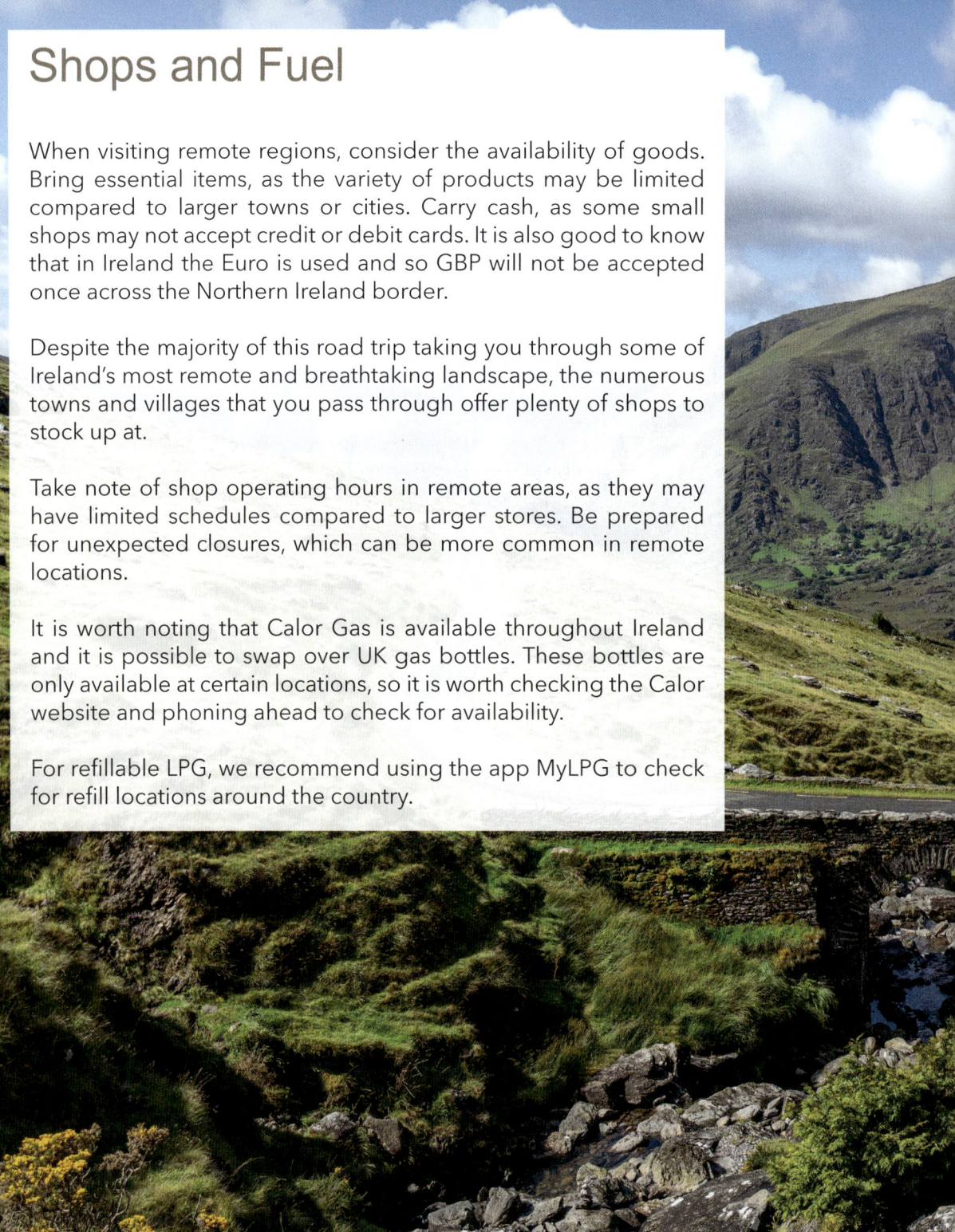

Shops and Fuel

When visiting remote regions, consider the availability of goods. Bring essential items, as the variety of products may be limited compared to larger towns or cities. Carry cash, as some small shops may not accept credit or debit cards. It is also good to know that in Ireland the Euro is used and so GBP will not be accepted once across the Northern Ireland border.

Despite the majority of this road trip taking you through some of Ireland's most remote and breathtaking landscape, the numerous towns and villages that you pass through offer plenty of shops to stock up at.

Take note of shop operating hours in remote areas, as they may have limited schedules compared to larger stores. Be prepared for unexpected closures, which can be more common in remote locations.

It is worth noting that Calor Gas is available throughout Ireland and it is possible to swap over UK gas bottles. These bottles are only available at certain locations, so it is worth checking the Calor website and phoning ahead to check for availability.

For refillable LPG, we recommend using the app MyLPG to check for refill locations around the country.

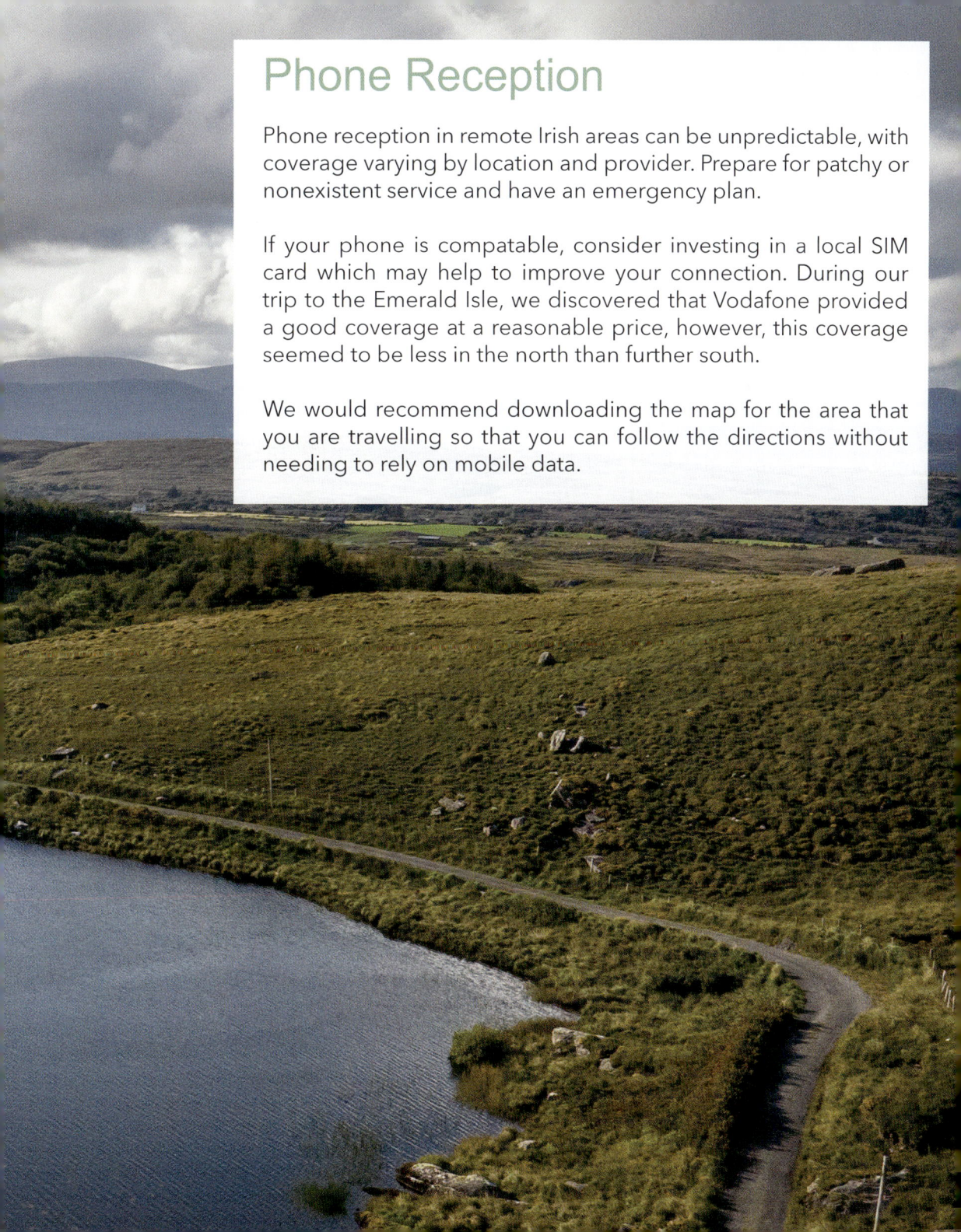

Phone Reception

Phone reception in remote Irish areas can be unpredictable, with coverage varying by location and provider. Prepare for patchy or nonexistent service and have an emergency plan.

If your phone is compatable, consider investing in a local SIM card which may help to improve your connection. During our trip to the Emerald Isle, we discovered that Vodafone provided a good coverage at a reasonable price, however, this coverage seemed to be less in the north than further south.

We would recommend downloading the map for the area that you are travelling so that you can follow the directions without needing to rely on mobile data.

Weather in Ireland

Weather in remote Irish areas can be unpredictable, with varying conditions depending on the time of year and location. Generally, Ireland's weather is influenced by the Atlantic Ocean, bringing cool, wet, and cloudy conditions, particularly in the west and northwest. However, weather can differ significantly based on elevation and proximity to the coast.

In summer, temperatures in remote areas can range from cool to warm, averaging from 15°C (59°F) to 20°C (68°F). Rain is possible, but sunny, pleasant days are also common. In winter, temperatures can be chilly, with average highs from 6°C (43°F) to 10°C (50°F). Frost, ice, and snow can occur, especially at higher elevations.

Preparing for various weather conditions is essential when visiting remote Irish areas. Pack warm clothing, waterproof gear, and sufficient water and snacks for unexpected delays. Being weather-ready ensures a safe and enjoyable trip, regardless of the forecast.

How Long Should You Spend on the Wild Atlantic Way?

The Wild Atlantic Way is an extraordinary coastal drive in Ireland, extending over 2,500 kilometres (1,550 miles) along the country's western shoreline. It presents the chance to discover some of Ireland's most breathtaking and pristine landscapes, from rugged cliffs and golden beaches to verdant hills and quaint villages.

Your time spent on the Wild Atlantic Way will depend on personal preferences and how much time you have. Some opt for a few days to explore a particular section, while others embark on a longer journey covering the entire route over a week or more.

We would suggest that if your time is limited, consider focusing on a specific region like the Southwest or Northwest. These areas provide a variety of experiences, from world-class surfing and mesmerising coastal drives to charming towns and villages. Alternatively, centre your trip on a particular activity like hiking or cycling which are both popular ways to travel along this coastal route.

Conversely, with more time available, a longer road trip covering the entire route from start to finish is worth considering.

The longer you have to enjoy this incredible part of the country the better as you will be able to travel at a slower pace and really soak up the beauty and culture along the way.

We have included a range of itineraries at the end of this book, perfect for planning your ultimate road trip. Spanning from 7 days to 4 weeks, these itineraries highlight the top sights recommended for each duration.

The Wild Side of the Wild Atlantic Way

Stretching along the rugged and captivating west coast of Ireland, the Wild Atlantic Way is an epic road trip that takes you on a journey through some of the most breathtaking landscapes in the world. The untamed beauty of the Atlantic Ocean crashes against towering cliffs, as the wind whispers through the untouched sands, creating a symphony that resonates with the soul.

It does not get much wilder than the Wild Atlantic Way in Ireland, with the unforgiving weather of the Atlantic Ocean that batter jagged cliffs and endless beaches of the western coastline. Thousands of years of this harsh environment is what has shaped this part of the world, and its people, into the beautiful and welcoming landscape and communities that you can enjoy all across Ireland.

94 SHANNON ESTUARY

90 KILKEE CLIFFS

Wild Camping on the Wild Atlantic Way

Ireland's rugged landscape, shaped by relentless weather over the centuries, offers ideal settings for diverse outdoor activities, including camping and hiking. The expansive wilderness regions throughout the country make "Wild" Camping (i.e., camping outside registered campsites) a common practice, particularly along the coastline and within national parks.

Imagine waking up in a secluded part of the world, the only sounds being your own breath, the wind rustling the tent, and possibly waves crashing on a nearby beach. Wild camping delivers an unparalleled experience for those seeking the raw and untamed side of nature.

It is crucial to note that Ireland does not have a Right to Roam, and as such it is important that you seek permission from the land owner before attempting any wild camping. Crossing fences or walls without permission is illegal, and land borders must be respected. However, certain regions in Ireland are more tolerant of camping, such as those near well-known hiking trails and within national parks with sparse habitation.

45 CEIDE FIELDS

64 DOOLOUGH VALLEY FAMINE MEMORIAL

Wild Swimming

Wild swimming evokes a sense of freedom and adventure. The icy cold water of Ireland's rugged western coast leaves you feeling alive and ready to face anything. Cold water relaxes the body and eases muscle aches while also boosting the immune system.

If you wish to enjoy a wild swim, whether it is your first time or you are a veteran, it is important to remember these crucial safety tips in order to enjoy the water safely. Swim with a partner for safety, and don't stay in until shivering, as this indicates the onset of hypothermia. Also, ensure you have warm layers to wear after swimming and bring a hot water bottle or hot drink to warm up immediately after swimming, as as the Atlantic Ocean water temperature means that hypothermia is a potential risk.

Be aware that wild swimming is at your own risk. Lifeguards are often present on beaches or pools in the West of Ireland, but cold temperatures pose a genuine hypothermia risk. Research safe swimming practices, always swim with a partner, and bring a flotation aid.

74 DOG'S BAY

Please be aware that you will do this at your own risk. There are not always lifeguards on duty the beaches or pools in Ireland and the cold temperature means that hypothermia is a real risk. Research how to swim safely, always swim with a partner, and take a flotation aid with you.

Safety When Swimming

Growing in popularity, wild swimming has revealed several overlooked safety factors in Ireland, such as rip currents, cold shock, and after drop. To stay safe while wild swimming, familiarise yourself with these terms and effective ways to mitigate these dangers, as they can lead to fatal consequences if left unaddressed.

Rip currents: More relevant to seaside swimming, rip currents are the tidal pull that leaves the shoreline between the swells. Once caught in a rip current, it becomes challenging to swim against the water flow pulling you out to sea. To escape, swim parallel to the shoreline until you are out of the rip, then swim towards the shore.

Cramps: Extreme cold can cause cramps during wild swimming. Don't panic if you experience cramps in your legs or arms. Your body is naturally buoyant, so call for help while lying on your back with your ears in the water. This position allows you to balance and float easily until rescued or the cramp disappears.

After drop: This is the continuous decline of your internal body temperature after leaving the water. Don't wait until shivering to leave the water, as this indicates hypothermia has begun.

Cold shock: The involuntary gasp and muscle seizure experienced when entering cold water can lead to drowning or pneumonia if the head is submerged. Enter the water slowly and acclimate before fully submerging.

Blood rush: After exiting the water, avoid jumping straight into a hot shower, as many cold-water swimmers end up fainting in the shower. The dilation of blood vessels in the outer extremities due to a sudden increase by external heat causes blood that has retreated to the body's core to rush back to the extremities, leaving a lack of blood in the brain and thus causing fainting.

Hiking on the Wild Atlantic Way

Hiking on the Wild Atlantic Way offers hikers many different types of terrain to explore: cliffs, forests, fields and mountains as well as beaches at either end of the trail. Hiking trails range from easy walks through wooded areas or along beaches (such as those found at Rossaveel) to more challenging hikes up higher peaks such as Carrauntoohil or Torc Mountain (where there are excellent views over Killarney National Park).

If you're looking for something even more challenging than hiking in Ireland's rugged landscape then Mount Brandon could be just what you're after - it features some steep climbs but also stunning views across Kerry's lakes region when you reach its summit.

Revered as Ireland's holiest peak, Croagh Patrick has been a pilgramige site for centuries and is a great mountain to climb in County Mayo.

62 CROAGH PATRICK

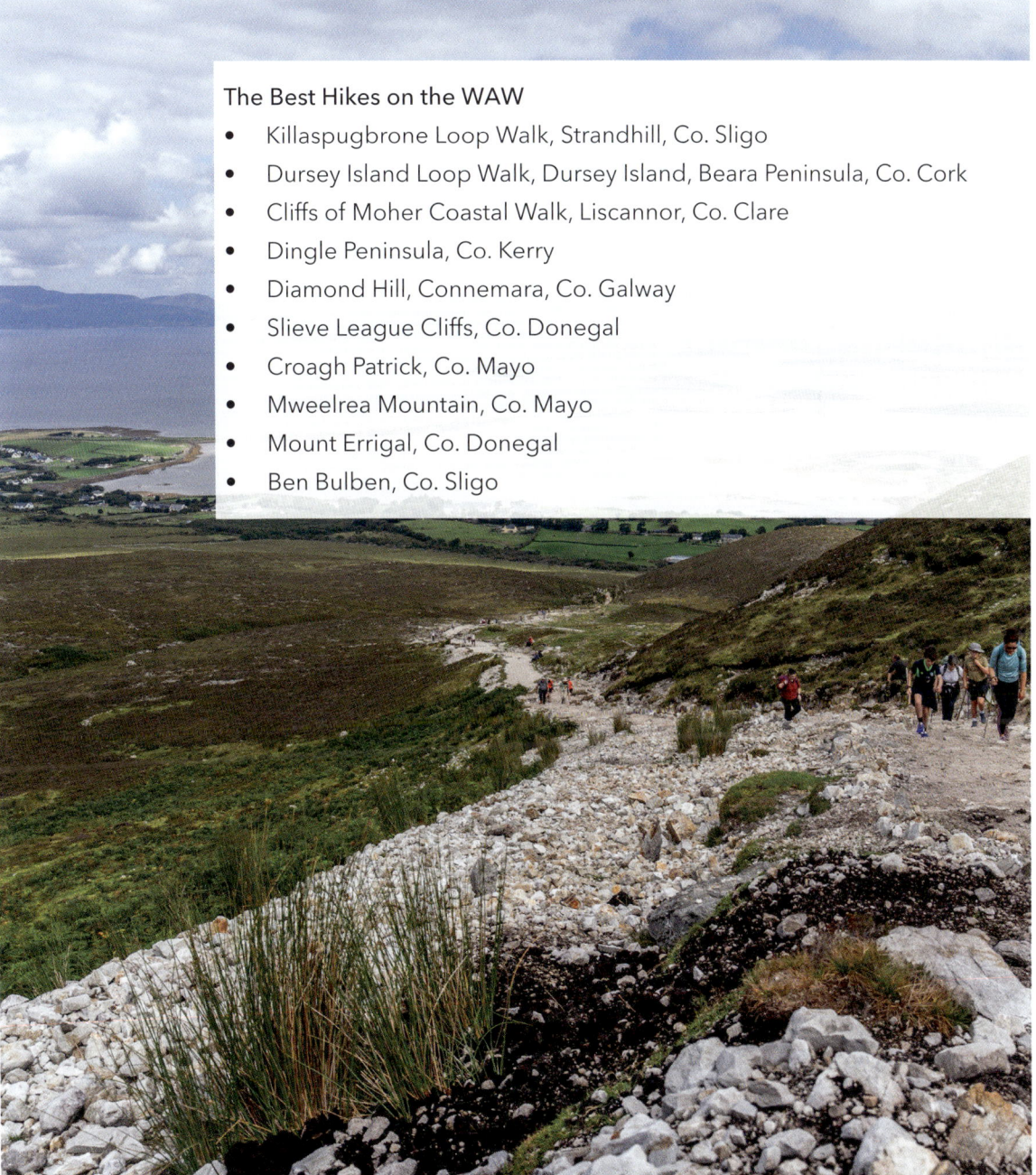

The Best Hikes on the WAW

- Killaspugbrone Loop Walk, Strandhill, Co. Sligo
- Dursey Island Loop Walk, Dursey Island, Beara Peninsula, Co. Cork
- Cliffs of Moher Coastal Walk, Liscannor, Co. Clare
- Dingle Peninsula, Co. Kerry
- Diamond Hill, Connemara, Co. Galway
- Slieve League Cliffs, Co. Donegal
- Croagh Patrick, Co. Mayo
- Mweelrea Mountain, Co. Mayo
- Mount Errigal, Co. Donegal
- Ben Bulben, Co. Sligo

Please be aware that you will do this at your own risk.
Hiking in Ireland can be a dangerous activity, with unpredictable weather systems and an isolated and remote countryside. Before you leave on any hike it is recommended that you pack for bad weather, bring a map and compass, and let someone know where you are going.

Essential Guidelines for Wild Activities
- Only camp where it is acceptable and with permission.
- Do not disturb the surrounding area and respect the locals. Remember you are their guest, act as such.
- When you leave the area make sure you leave nothing but footprints and take nothing but memories! This is the biggest crime you can do while wild camping and is the main reason it is becoming illegal.
- Bury your waste (including the toilet paper, or carry a bag to dispose of it in). Don't leave your business lying around.
- Do not overstay your welcome. Arriving after dark and leaving before light will ensure that people can continue to use these areas without complaints.

Responsibly Wild

The Wild Atlantic Way in Ireland is a unique and awe-inspiring destination. The remote and rugged terrain is home to a wide variety of flora and fauna, from wildflowers to seabirds, and provides a glimpse into the natural world as it was meant to be.

As more and more people discover the beauty of the WAW, it's important to remember our responsibility to protect and preserve this stunning environment. This means treading lightly and leaving no trace, so that future generations can continue to enjoy the beauty of the Irish coastline.

Whether you're hiking, cycling, or simply taking a leisurely drive, there are countless opportunities to appreciate the natural beauty of the WAW. From the towering sea cliffs of Donegal to the windswept beaches of Kerry, there's something for everyone along this incredible route.

But as we enjoy the wild beauty of the WAW, we must also remember that we are guests in this natural environment. It's up to each of us to do our part to protect the landscape and ensure that it remains pristine for years to come. So as you explore the Wild Atlantic Way, take a moment to appreciate the natural wonders around you, and do your part to preserve them for future generations. Together, we can all play a role in protecting this unique and precious resource.

3 MALIN HEAD

Best of the Wild Atlantic Way

In a world that seems to be getting smaller every day, the Wild Atlantic Way in Ireland offers a refreshing reminder that there are still vast and untamed corners of the world waiting to be explored. From the windswept beaches of Donegal to the rugged cliffs of Kerry, the WAW invites you to embark on a journey of discovery, where each new turn in the road brings fresh wonders to behold.

In this age of instant gratification and digital distractions, the WAW offers a welcome escape from the noise and clutter of modern life. With its breathtaking landscapes, stunning seascapes, and hidden gems waiting to be uncovered, the WAW provides a rare opportunity to slow down, switch off, and connect with the natural world in a profound and meaningful way.

Whether you're an intrepid adventurer seeking out the wild and remote corners of the Emerald Isle or a curious traveller eager to immerse yourself in the rich culture and history of Ireland's west coast, the Wild Atlantic Way is an experience that will leave you breathless and longing for more.

Upon the rugged coast of green,
Where waves crash wild and free,
There lies a land of ancient dreams,
As proud as it can be.

The craggy cliffs and rocky shore,
Stand steadfast through the years,
Reflecting in their rugged form,
A people filled with cheers.

From north to south, from east to west,
The land is steeped in lore,
With stories told of battles fought,
And heroes gone before.

So here's a toast to Ireland fair,
And all its rugged coast,
May we cherish every corner,
And raise a hearty toast.

- Source Unknown

Best Distilleries to Visit on the Wild Atlantic Way

- Dingle Distillery - County Kerry
- Clonakilty Distillery - County Cork
- West Cork Distillers - County Cork
- Connacht Whiskey Company - County Mayo
- The Shed Distillery of PJ Rigney - County Leitrim
- Achill Island Distillery - County Mayo (currently in development)
- Lough Mask Distillery - County Mayo (currently in development)
- Micil Distillery - Galway City, County Galway
- The Burren Brewery - Lisdoonvarna, County Clare
- Western Herd Brewery - Ennis, County Clare
- White Hag Brewery - Ballymote, County Sligo
- Lough Gill Distillery - Sligo, County Sligo
- Cape Clear Distillery - Cape Clear, Cork

Drink driving is illegal in Ireland. If you are driving around the Wild Atlantic Way then it is important to highlight that NO ALCOHOL should be consumed before driving in Ireland. Due to the low legal limit in Ireland, it is also recommended that you wait 24hrs after drinking before driving.

Best Distilleries & Breweries
on the Wild Atlantic Way

What better place is there to sample a taste of Ireland's most famous product; the smooth, complex, and rich Irish Whiskey, and the crisp, refreshing, and flavourful Irish craft beer? The wild Atlantic coast of Ireland is home to an array of distilleries and breweries, each with their own unique story and flavour profile to tell. From the rugged coastline of County Kerry to the stunning beaches of County Clare, the west coast of Ireland is a haven for whiskey and beer enthusiasts alike.

The production of Irish whiskey and craft beer is steeped in tradition and history, with each distillery and brewery having their own way of doing things that have been passed down through generations. From the locally-sourced ingredients to the careful ageing process, every step of the production process is integral to the final product.

Tours of these distilleries and breweries are a must for anyone visiting the west coast of Ireland, providing an opportunity to learn about the history and production of these iconic Irish beverages. Many offer tastings of their signature products, allowing visitors to sample the unique flavours and aromas that each location has to offer.

Obviously, if you are driving then you will not be able to partake in this final tasting, however, fear not as a lot of distilleries offer sample kits to be taken away and enjoyed later in the evening instead.

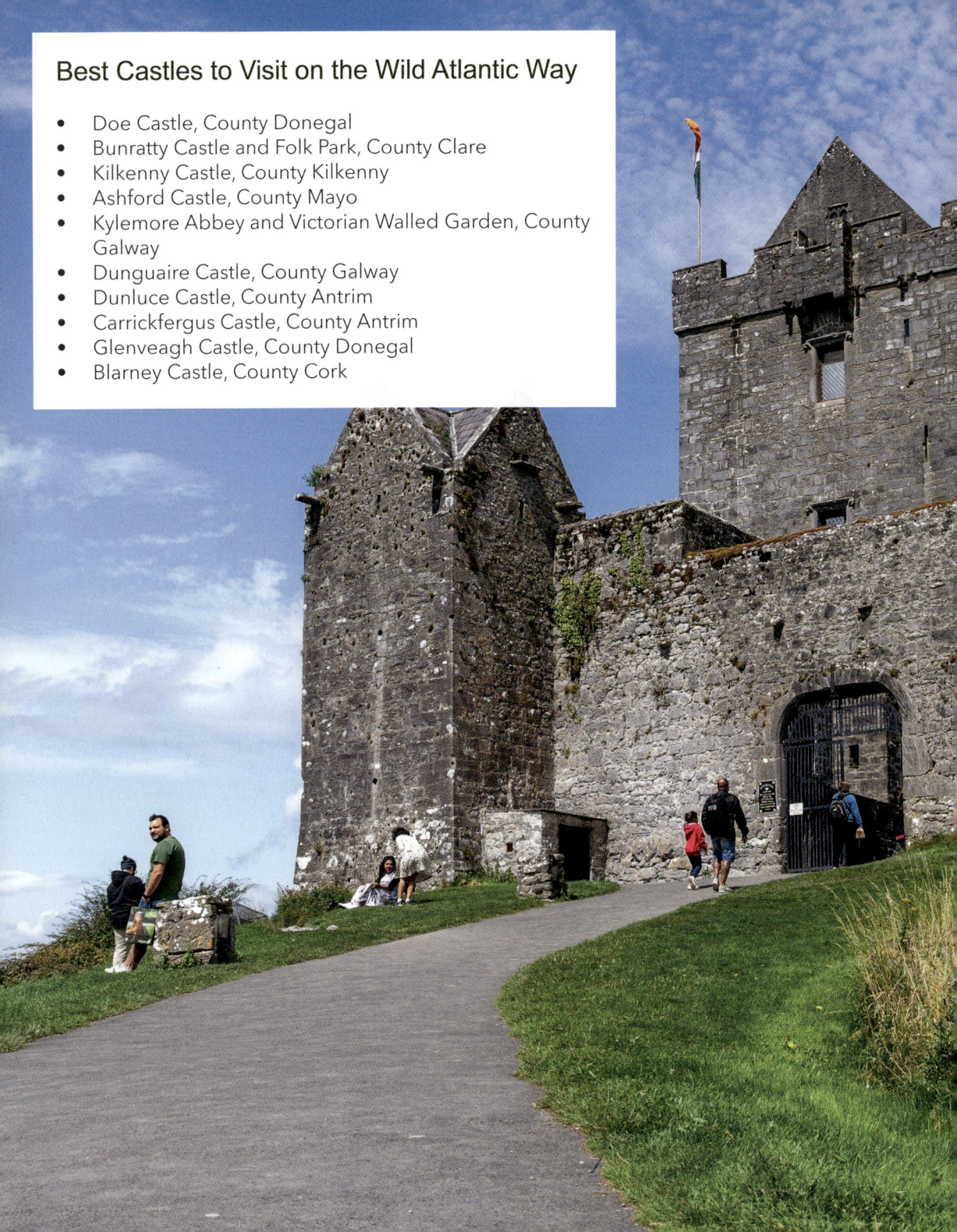

Best Castles to Visit on the Wild Atlantic Way

- Doe Castle, County Donegal
- Bunratty Castle and Folk Park, County Clare
- Kilkenny Castle, County Kilkenny
- Ashford Castle, County Mayo
- Kylemore Abbey and Victorian Walled Garden, County Galway
- Dunguaire Castle, County Galway
- Dunluce Castle, County Antrim
- Carrickfergus Castle, County Antrim
- Glenveagh Castle, County Donegal
- Blarney Castle, County Cork

Best Castles
on the Wild Atlantic Way

Of all the things to see on the Wild Atlantic Way, few are as impressive and magnificent as the castles that dot the coastline. These ancient fortresses, built centuries ago to protect against invading armies, are a testament to the resilience and ingenuity of the people who once called this rugged land home.

The castles on the Wild Atlantic Way come in all shapes and sizes, from the towering ruins of mediaeval fortresses to the stately homes of wealthy aristocrats. Each one has its own unique story to tell, and exploring these ancient structures is a fascinating journey through time.

Some of the most famous castles on the Wild Atlantic Way include the majestic Kylemore Abbey, a beautiful neo-Gothic structure set amidst the stunning Connemara landscape, and the imposing ruins of Donegal Castle, which once served as the stronghold of the powerful O'Donnell clan.

Other must-see castles along the route include the stunning Blarney Castle, home to the famous Blarney Stone, and the dramatic Dunluce Castle, perched precariously on a rocky outcrop overlooking the turbulent waters of the North Atlantic.

Whether you're a history buff or just appreciate the beauty and grandeur of these ancient structures, the castles of the Wild Atlantic Way are sure to leave a lasting impression. So pack your bags, hit the road, and prepare to be transported back in time as you explore the rich and storied history of Ireland's wild west coast.

Best Mountains to Visit on the Wild Atlantic Way

- Croagh Patrick - located in County Mayo
- Mount Errigal - located in County Donegal
- Mweelrea - located in County Mayo
- Benbulbin - located in County Sligo
- Diamond Hill - located in Connemara, County Galway
- Knocknarea - located in County Sligo
- Brandon Mountain - located in County Kerry
- Sliabh Liag - located in County Donegal
- Macgillycuddy's Reeks - located in County Kerry
- Twelve Bens - located in Connemara, County Galway
- Nephin Range - located in County Mayo
- Ox Mountains - located in County Sligo
- Dartry Mountains - located in County Mayo
- Bluestack Mountains - located in County Mayo
- Sheeffry Hills - located in County Mayo

Best Mountains
on the Wild Atlantic Way

The rugged and untamed coastline of the Wild Atlantic Way tells a story of unfathomable strength, power, and resilience. Over millions of years, relentless tides, unyielding winds, and crashing waves have carved out dramatic cliffs, deep fjords, and towering sea stacks. The sheer force of nature is visible in every nook and cranny of this epic coastal route, as jagged rocks jut out from the roiling Atlantic and storms rage overhead.

It is a story that began millions of years ago, when the relentless force of the Atlantic Ocean shaped and moulded the landscape into what we see today. From the jagged cliffs of Donegal's Sliabh Liag to the rolling waves of Kerry's Dingle Peninsula, the raw and untamed beauty of this coastline is truly awe-inspiring.

Each rocky outcrop and steep cliff face has a unique story to tell, from the ancient geological events that shaped the land to the rich history and folklore of the people who have lived and worked along the coast for generations. The Wild Atlantic Way is a journey through time, an exploration of the very essence of Ireland's rugged and unyielding coastline.

As you travel along the route, you will be struck by the sheer majesty of the landscape, as towering cliffs give way to sandy beaches and secluded coves. It is a journey that takes you from the highest peaks of the mountains to the depths of the ocean, revealing hidden treasures at every turn.

Best Waterfalls to Visit on the Wild Atlantic Way

- Torc Waterfall
- Gleninchaquin Waterfall
- O'Sullivan's Cascade
- The Cliffs of Moher Waterfall
- Aasleagh Falls
- Sruth in Aghaidh An Aird (The Devil's Chimney)
- Glencar Waterfall
- Assaranca Waterfall
- Cloghaneely Waterfall
- Cloghane Cascade

Best Waterfalls
on the Wild Atlantic Way

The Wild Atlantic Way is home to some of the rainiest and windiest weather in Europe, with some areas experiencing over 200 days of rain a year. This infamous grey weather is brought by the prevailing winds from the Atlantic Ocean, which constantly batter the coastline, bringing with them an endless stream of rain and mist.

The mountains of Connemara, Donegal and Kerry bear the brunt of these wild conditions, and as a result, the area is home to some of the most stunning waterfalls in the world. These falls, such as the breathtaking Siabh Liag, cascade down from dizzying heights, creating a symphony of sound and motion that has to be seen to be believed. The unrelenting weather and rugged terrain of the west coast may be harsh, but it has carved out a landscape that is truly awe-inspiring.

Waterfalls such as the Glencar Waterfall in County Leitrim and the Torc Waterfall in Killarney National Park can be found along the length of Ireland's western coast. These cascading waterfalls are truly breathtaking, and are often surrounded by rugged, rocky terrain that adds to their dramatic beauty. With so much rainfall in the region, it's no wonder that the west coast of Ireland boasts some of the most spectacular waterfalls in the world.

Best Beaches to Visit on the Wild Atlantic Way

- Keem Bay, Achill Island, County Mayo
- Kinnagoe Bay, County Donegal
- Banna Strand, County Kerry
- Lahinch Beach, County Clare
- Inchydoney Beach, County Cork
- Salthill Beach, County Galway
- Rosses Point Beach, County Sligo
- Fanad Head Beach, County Donegal
- Barleycove Beach, County Cork
- Derrynane Beach, County Kerry
- White Strand, County Clare

Best Beaches
on the Wild Atlantic Way

Stretching over 2500 km in length, the Wild Atlantic Way is a coastal route along the western seaboard of Ireland that is just as rugged and awe-inspiring as the Scottish coastline. The endless stretches of sand dunes, the soaring cliffs, and the rolling waves crashing against the rocks make it a paradise for nature lovers and outdoor enthusiasts alike.

There are over a dozen Blue Flag beaches on the Wild Atlantic Way, each with its unique charm and character. From the windswept Rossbeigh beach to the tranquil Silver Strand in County Mayo, each beach has something special to offer. You can spend hours walking along the beaches, listening to the sound of the waves, and taking in the stunning views of the ocean.

If you're feeling brave, you can take a dip in the ocean and enjoy a refreshing swim in the crystal-clear water. While the water may be chilly, it is an invigorating and unforgettable experience. You can also try your hand at surfing, kiteboarding, or sea kayaking at some of the more popular beaches along the route.

Many Irish beaches have lifeguards on duty during the summer months to ensure the safety of swimmers and beachgoers. These trained professionals keep a watchful eye on the water and provide assistance to those in need. Their presence gives visitors peace of mind and allows them to fully enjoy their day at the beach. It's important to always follow the advice of lifeguards and pay attention to warning flags or signs to stay safe in the water.

Whether you're looking for a peaceful, secluded cove or a lively, family-friendly beach, the Wild Atlantic Way has it all. So pack your bags, grab your swimwear, and get ready for an adventure along one of the most beautiful coastlines in the world.

NOTE - A blue flag beach in Ireland is an award given to beaches that meet high standards of water quality and safety.

SIGHTS

Beaches & Harbours
1. Stroove beach
2. Kinnagoe Bay
4. Trawbreaga Bay
5. Five Finger Strand
8. Pollan Strand
9. Tullagh Bay
13. Lisfannon Beach

Viewpoints
3. Malin Head
11. Gap of Mamore
12. Dunree Head

Island
6. Isle of Doagh
14. Inch Island

Castles & Historical Sights
7. Carrickabraghy Castle
15. Derry Walls

Waterfalls
10. Glenevin Waterfall

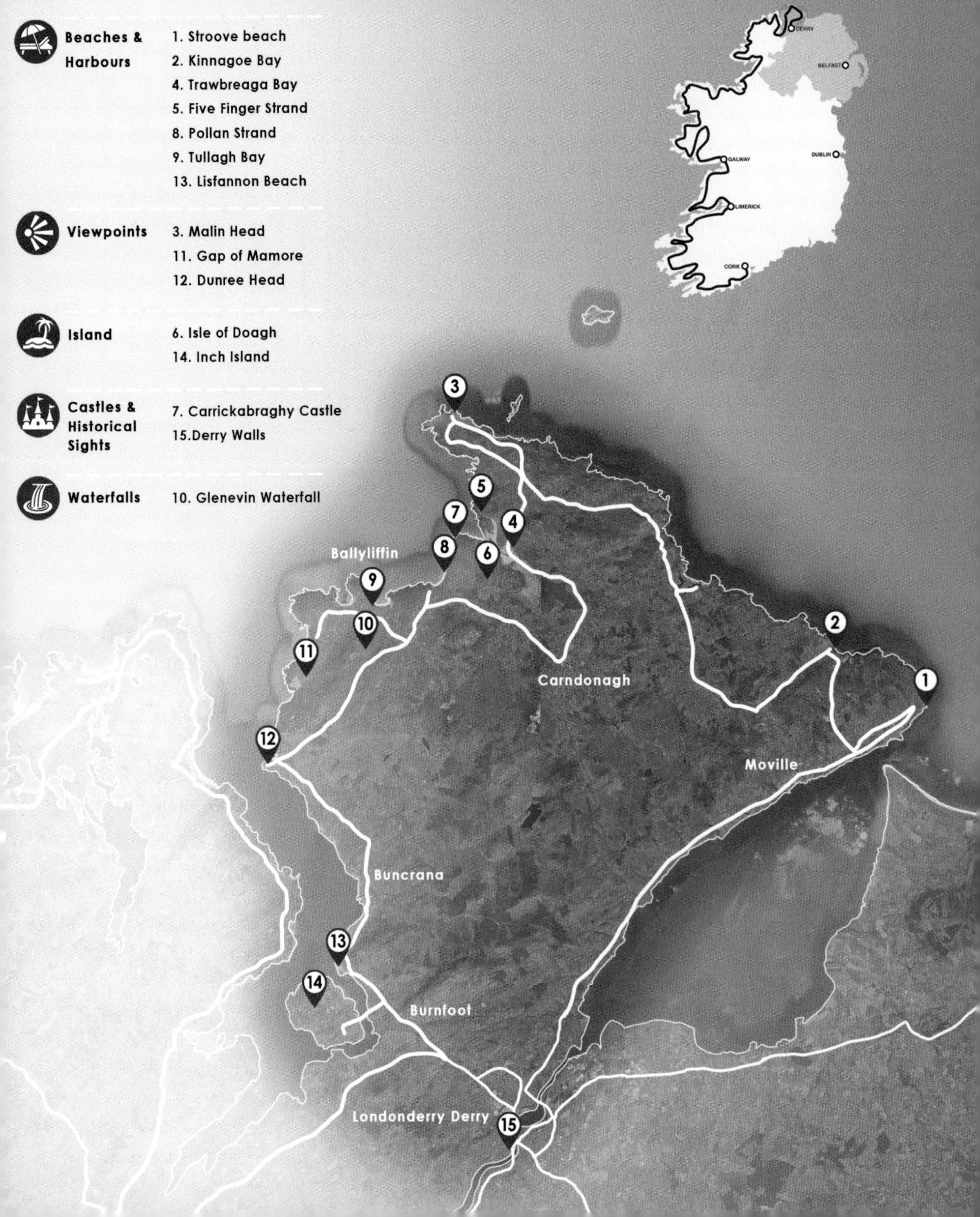

Inishowen Peninsula

The Inishowen Peninsula is a place of legends and lore, steeped in history and culture. It is said that this part of Ireland was once the stronghold of the mythical warrior race, the Tuatha Dé Danann, who were said to have ruled the land with their magical powers. As you travel through the region, you will see evidence of the area's rich heritage at every turn, from ancient stone circles to ruined castles and medieval churches.

The Inishowen Peninsula is more than just a place of history and myth. It is also home to some of the most breathtaking scenery in Ireland. From the rugged cliffs of Malin Head, the most northerly point in Ireland, to the peaceful waters of Lough Swilly, the natural beauty of this region is simply breathtaking.

One of the most remarkable aspects of the Inishowen Peninsula is the diversity of its landscape. The rolling hills that dominate the peninsula's interior give way to a rugged coastline, where towering cliffs and secluded coves are carved into the landscape. It is the perfect place for outdoor enthusiasts, who come to hike, cycle, and kayak along the coast, exploring hidden beaches and secret coves along the way.

Lastly, of course, there are the beaches. From the long, sweeping sands of Lagg Beach to the secluded bay of Portsalon, the Inishowen Peninsula boasts some of the most beautiful beaches in Ireland. But it's not just the sand and surf that draw visitors to these shores - it's the feeling of peace and tranquillity that comes from being surrounded by such stunning natural beauty.

In order to reach Inishowen Peninsula, the closest airport is in Londonderry/Derry, where you will also find train links from other major cities. You can also rent a car or catch public transport from here out to the peninsula.

5 FIVE FINGER STRAND

The Inishowen Peninsula is a place of contrasts - a land of rugged beauty and gentle tranquillity, of ancient legends and modern culture. Whether you're a history buff, an outdoor enthusiast, or simply looking for a place to relax and unwind, this is a destination that will capture your heart and leave you with memories that will last a lifetime.

For those seeking a taste of Irish culture, the Inishowen Peninsula has plenty to offer. From traditional music sessions in local pubs to the vibrant festivals that take place throughout the year, there is always something to see and do in this part of Ireland. In addition to this, there is the warmth and hospitality of the local people, who will make you feel welcome wherever you go.

1. Stroove Beach

Stroove Beach is a sheltered bay on the Inishowen Peninsula offering a peaceful escape with stunning views of the Atlantic Ocean and the Scottish Isles in the distance. Known for its crystal-clear waters, perfect for swimming or kayaking, and its soft white sands are perfect for a relaxing stroll or a picnic.

The Sea View Sauna is also only 50m from the sea which you may wish to try out after a cold dip. There is ample parking and toilet facilities.

-> Follow the R238 and then the R241 road towards Greencastle and continue past this town to the Inishowen Head Lighthouse. Wheelchair accessible. Dog-friendly. ///skis.depart.checklist

2. Kinnagoe Bay

This secluded beach boasts crystal-clear turquoise water, soft white sand, and dramatic cliffs that surround the bay, creating a stunning natural amphitheatre.

The beach is relatively small, but its intimate size only adds to the charm and peacefulness of the area. Whether you're looking to take a dip in the refreshing water, stroll along the shore, or simply relax and soak in the breathtaking scenery, Kinnagoe Bay is the perfect destination for a day trip or a longer stay on the Emerald Isle.

-> Follow the R238 and R241 roads towards Greencastle, then continue past the town to the Inishowen Head Lighthouse. Dog-friendly. ///burden.leaped.pocketing

3. Malin Head

Located on the Inishowen Peninsula in County Donegal, Malin Head is the most northerly point of Ireland and is renowned for its rugged and wild beauty. This stunning destination is a popular spot for tourists and locals alike, offering panoramic views of the Atlantic Ocean and the dramatic coastline. Visitors can take a leisurely stroll along the cliff tops or explore the many walking trails that weave through the area, taking in the striking scenery along the way.

For those seeking adventure, Malin Head is a popular spot for water sports such as surfing and kayaking. It is also home to a wealth of fascinating history and folklore, with many ancient ruins and monuments dotted throughout the area. A visit to Malin Head is a must for anyone exploring the wild and untamed beauty of the Inishowen Peninsula.

-> From Letterkenny, follow the R244 to Malin village and then continue to Malin Head. It's a 1 hour 45 minute drive from Derry and about 1 hour from Letterkenny. Wheelchair accessible. Dog-friendly. ///immediate.parole.tigers

3 MALIN HEAD

4. Trawbreaga Bay

Nestled on the northern coast of County Donegal, this hidden gem is known for its stunning natural beauty and peaceful atmosphere. Trawbreaga Bay boasts a long stretch of sandy beach and clear blue waters.

The bay is a popular spot for fishing and water sports, as well as leisurely walks along the shoreline. It is a serene escape from the hustle and bustle of everyday life, and the perfect place to unwind and connect with nature.

-> Take the R238 north from Derry/Londonderry or the R244 from Letterkenny to Carndonagh. From Carndonagh, take the R238 towards Culdaff and look for signs for Trawbreaga Bay. Dog-friendly.
///extra.beeline.unlike

5. Five Finger Strand

Located in the Inishowen Peninsula in County Donegal, this beach offers stunning views of the Atlantic Ocean and the surrounding cliffs. The beach is known for its dramatic landscape, with large rock formations and caves to explore. It's a popular spot for swimmers, but also offers plenty of space for those looking to relax and soak up the sun. The beach is easily accessible by car and has a small carpark. Not suitable for motorhomes.

-> Head north on the R238 from Derry/Londonderry or take the R244 from Letterkenny to Carndonagh. From Carndonagh, follow the R238 towards Malin and look for signs for Five Finger Strand. Dog-friendly.
///fundraiser.headquarters.lifeboat

5 FIVE FINGER STRAND

5 FIVE FINGER STRAND

6. Isle of Doagh

The Isle of Doagh, located on the Inishowen Peninsula in County Donegal, is a picturesque area surrounded by rugged coastline and stunning beaches. It is home to a variety of outdoor activities such as fishing, kayaking, and hiking. Visitors can explore the Famine Village, which provides a glimpse into the harsh living conditions endured by families during the Irish Potato Famine in the 1840s. The island also offers breathtaking views of the Atlantic Ocean, with ample opportunities to witness the vibrant sunsets and local wildlife.

-> Take the R238 from Derry/Londonderry or the R244 from Letterkenny to Carndonagh. From Carndonagh, take the R238 towards Ballyliffin and follow the signs to the Isle of Doagh. Wheelchair accessible. Dog-friendly.
 ///disagree.heave.convergent

6 | ISLE OF DOAGH

7. Carrickabraghy Castle

Perched atop a rocky outcrop overlooking the wild Atlantic Ocean, this castle ruins are a testament to the turbulent history of the region. The castle dates back to the early 16th century and was built by the powerful MacSuibhne clan. It played a key role in various battles over the centuries, including the Nine Years War, and was eventually abandoned in the 18th century. Despite its ruined state, the castle's imposing walls and commanding views are a must-see for any visitor to the area.

-> Take the R238 north from Londonderry or the R244 from Letterkenny to Carndonagh. Follow the R240 towards Greencastle and watch for signs for Carrickabraghy Castle. It's a 20min drive from Carndonagh to Carrickabraghy Castle. Dog-friendly. ///prohibited.mooring.ballroom

7 CARRICKABRAGHY CASTLE

9 TULLAGH BAY

8. Pollan Strand

As you stroll along the rugged coastline of the Inishowen peninsula, you'll come across a breathtaking expanse of white sand known as Pollan Strand. Whether you're looking to take a refreshing dip in the sea, to take a stroll along the shore, or to simply relax and soak up the stunning views, this stretch of beach is the perfect place to unwind and escape from the stresses of everyday life. With its pristine sands, crystal clear waters, and breathtaking scenery, it's no wonder that this beach is a favourite among locals and tourists alike.

-> *Take the R238 north from Derry/Londonderry or the R244 from Letterkenny to Buncrana. From Buncrana, follow the signs for Fahan and make your way to the R238. Continue on the R238 towards Ballyliffin and look for signs for Pollan Strand. Dog-friendly. ///pressuring. spires.contingent*

9. Tullagh Bay

Nestled along the Wild Atlantic Way, a hidden gem awaits you at Tullagh Bay. The vast expanse of golden sand and clear blue waters will take your breath away. It's hard not to feel a sense of peace and tranquillity as you walk along the shore, with only the sound of waves lapping against the sand to accompany you. With its stunning backdrop of rugged cliffs and rolling hills, Tullagh Bay is a paradise for nature lovers and adventure seekers alike. Whether you're looking to surf, swim, or simply bask in the beauty of your surroundings, Tullagh Bay is a must-visit destination.

-> *From Ballyliffin, head north on R238/N13 road for about 6 kilometers until you reach Tullagh Bay. Look for signs or landmarks indicating the entrance to the bay. Dog-friendly. ///dented.mended.implies*

10. Glenevin Waterfall

Surrounded by lush greenery and towering trees, a hidden gem awaits in the form of a majestic waterfall. The Glenevin Waterfall, located in the heart of Inishowen Peninsula, Ireland, is a breathtaking sight to behold. The cascading water flows over rocky terrain, creating a symphony of soothing sounds that can be heard from a distance. Visitors can take a leisurely hike through the forest to reach the falls and enjoy a picnic on the nearby benches while taking in the tranquil scenery. The Glenevin Waterfall is truly a natural wonder that captivates the senses and leaves a lasting impression.

-> Located on the road that sits between Clonmany and Kindrohid. Large car park and donation based. Wheelchair accessible. ///illnesses.elects.alcoves

10 GLENEVIN WATERFALL

11. Gap of Mamore

As you journey through the winding mountain roads, you suddenly reach a vast opening in the hills - the breathtaking Gap of Mamore. The scenery here is nothing short of spectacular, with majestic mountains rising up on both sides and a winding road leading through the valley. It's a place that truly leaves you in awe of the natural beauty of Ireland. The gap has been formed over thousands of years by a glacier, leaving behind a unique and awe-inspiring landscape.

-> Follow the R238/N13 road and turn at the sign for Mamore Gap. Travel for 3kms until you reach the parking area and enjoy the scenic views. Be aware of the winding roads and use caution when driving. Wheelchair accessible. Dog-friendly. ///vans.committing.flickering

11 GAP OF MAMORE

12. Dunree Head
Perched high above the swirling Atlantic Ocean, this rugged headland offers panoramic views of the surrounding coastline. The sight of crashing waves against the sheer cliffs below is both awe-inspiring and humbling. This historic site was once home to a military fortification, and remnants of the past can still be seen in the form of rusted cannons and abandoned bunkers. The bracing sea air and stunning natural beauty make Dunree Head a must-visit for anyone exploring the Inishowen Peninsula.

-> *Follow the R238/N13 road towards Dunree Military Museum. Continue along this road until you reach Dunree Head. Look for signs indicating the entrance to the headland. Wheelchair accessible. Dog-friendly. ///racing.honks.stormed*

13. Lisfannon Beach
With its vast expanse of golden sand and crystal-clear waters, this beach is a paradise for beach-goers and water sport enthusiasts alike. The sweeping views of the majestic mountains and the soothing sound of the waves make for a truly serene atmosphere.

The beach is also steeped in history, with ancient ruins and artifacts found nearby, offering a glimpse into the region's rich past. Whether you're looking for a peaceful escape or an exciting adventure, this beach has something for everyone to enjoy.

-> *Lisfannon Beach is accessible through the R238 road and is set beneath low dunes that dominate its carpark. Dog-friendly. ///soliciting.wrestling.storms*

12 DUNREE HEAD

14. Inch Island

Nestled in the picturesque Lough Swilly, this tranquil island offers a serene escape from the hustle and bustle of everyday life. Surrounded by crystal-clear waters and panoramic views, it's the perfect place to unwind and soak up the natural beauty of the area.

With plenty of hiking trails and wildlife to observe, it's a nature lover's paradise. The island's historic past is also evident, with the ruins of an old castle and an ancient graveyard to explore.

-> Take the Buncrana Rd from north Londonderry and turn right at Bridge End onto the R238. Take a left at Rockhead onto Inch Road and follow this across the casuseway onto the island. Wheelchair accessible. Dog-friendly.
///legroom.notify.merger

15. Derry Walls

Standing tall and proud, the ancient walls of this historic city are a sight to behold. Built in the 17th century, they have withstood centuries of tumultuous history, and bear the scars of numerous battles. The walls offer a glimpse into the past, taking visitors on a journey through time. As you walk along the ramparts, you can almost feel the weight of the city's history, and the stories it has to tell. The views from the top are breathtaking, and offer a unique perspective of the city and its surroundings.

-> The walls sit around the centre of the old city. From the River Foyle, head northwest along Carlisle Rd, Hawkin St, London St, and Society St to reach the Royal Bastion. Wheelchair Accessible. Dog-friendly.
///aside.ages.smug

15 DERRY WALLS

Where to Eat
on the Inishowen Peninsula

Scarpello & Co Bakehouse & Pizzeria
Located on Buncrana Road, their menu boasts a tempting selection of Artisan bread and woodfired pizza. With a cosy ambiance and friendly staff, it's a must-visit for food lovers in the area.

-> BT48 8AB. ///ticket.angle.fears

The Railway Tavern
A charming pub perfect for unwinding after a long day. Visitors can indulge in a pint of locally brewed ale or relax with a coffee in the cosy outdoor seating area. The tavern also features a pool table and live music, creating a vibrant atmosphere for guests.

-> F93 TVF2. Wheelchair Accessible. ///hosted.flung.concentration

Claire the Bakers
Known for their fresh, homemade pastries, breads, and cakes, Claire's offers a delectable range of treats to satisfy any sweet tooth. With friendly staff and a warm atmosphere, it's a must-visit for bakery enthusiasts in the area.

-> F93 V2ND. Wheelchair Accessible. ///cycle.aero.resembled

McGrory's Hotel Culdaff
A charming coastal retreat that offers a wonderful blend of comfort and relaxation. With comfortable rooms, a cosy pub, and a renowned restaurant, guests can enjoy a memorable stay. The hotel also hosts live music events, making it a hub for entertainment in the area.

-> F93 TP9N. Wheelchair Accessible. ///milder.adults.mottos

Caffe Banbha Malin Head
Perched at the edge of the world, this small coffee box offers the most spectacular place to enjoy a fresh brew and a sweet treat. This van has been serving tourists fresh baked goods and warming drinks for 15 years, ensuring that all visitors to Malin Head leave refreshed, refueled, and ready for their next adventure.

-> F93 D2R4. Wheelchair Accessible. Dog-friendly. ///success.liberating.washed

The Rusty Nail
With its rustic decor and warm hospitality, it's the perfect place to unwind and enjoy a pint of Guinness. Live music performances and a hearty menu of pub food further enhance the memorable experience at The Rusty Nail.

-> F93 R927. Wheelchair Accessible. ///twitter.forewarned.twice

3 MALIN HEAD

Where to Stay
on the Inishowen Peninsula

Hotels
- Bishop's Gate Hotel Derry (Wheelchair Accessible)
- The Waterfoot Hotel (Wheelchair Accessible)
- Art House
- Redcastle Hotel (Wheelchair Accessible)
- Crag Na Cor B&B

Self-Catering Apartments
- Lissadell Holiday Apartment (Dog-friendly)
- Rosebank Apartments
- 25 Millers Way
- Beechwood, Londonderry

Campsites

Foyleside Caravan Park
A family-run park offers picturesque views of Lough Foyle and the majestic Coleraine mountains. Foyleside is the perfect base for exploring the beautiful Donegal region, Ireland's northernmost peninsula.

-> F93 KHH1. ///tourism.finals.remotes

Binion Bay Caravan & Camping Facility
Nestled in the rugged coastline of Donegal, Binion Bay Caravan & Camping Facility offers stunning sea views, a tranquil atmosphere, and a range of outdoor activities for all ages.

-> F93 R927. Wheelchair Accessible. Dog friendly. ///twitter.forewarned.twice

Roadtrip Essentials
on the Inishowen Peninsula

Food Shops
- Tesco, Londonderry
- Lidl, Londonderry
- Sainsburys, Londonderry
- Spar, Burnfoot
- Aldi, Buncrana
- Supervalu, Carndonagh

Water Points and CDP
- Bridgend Service Station (Water only)
- Stroove Beach (Water only)
- Carndonagh Car Park (CDP & Water)
- Buncrana Tourist Info (CDP & Water)

Electric Vehicle Charging Points
- Monta Charging Point, Ballyliffin Golf Club ///motors.experienced.marzipan
- EBS Charging Point, Bridge Street ///fossil.slogs.wordplay
- Tesla Destination Charger, Redcastle Hotel ///thunder.admittedly.smear
- eCars Charge Point, Nailor's Row ///shadowing.sweaty.roadhous
- ESB ecars Charging Station, Carlisle Road ///bank.fortunate.pets
- ecars Charging Point, Bishop Street ///palm.trash.direct

9 TULLAGH BAY

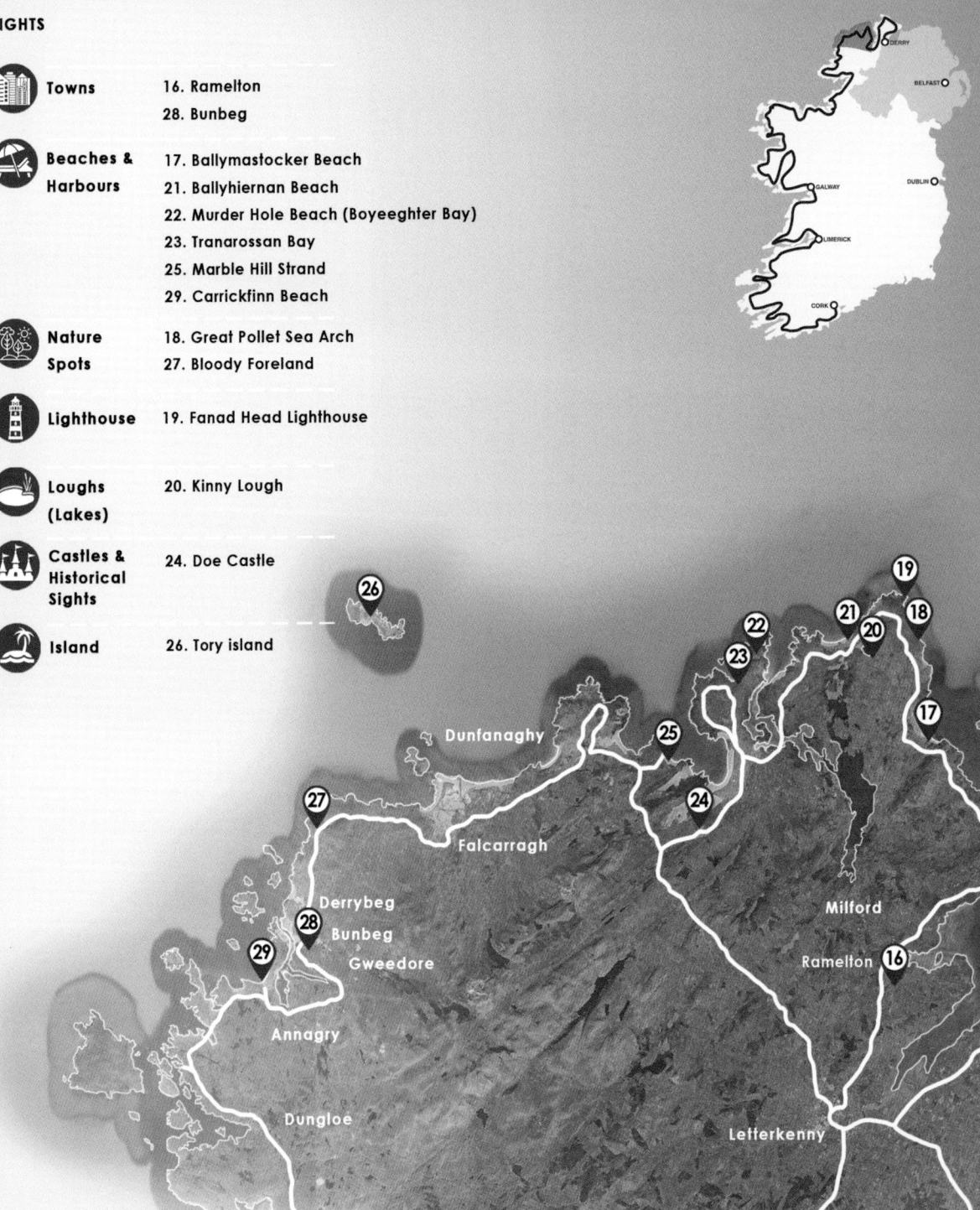

Fanad Head

On the captivating northwestern corner of the Wild Atlantic Way lies the Fanad Peninsula, an intriguing destination where nature showcases its unbridled splendour. The Fanad Peninsula, steeped in folklore and cultural richness, allows visitors to delve into Ireland's storied past through its ancient artifacts, crumbling castles, and centuries-old churches.

Beyond its historical allure, the Fanad Peninsula boasts some of Ireland's most incredible landscapes. From the imposing Fanad Head Lighthouse, which guards the peninsula's northernmost point, to the serene waters of Mulroy Bay, the area's beauty is truly unparalleled.

The Fanad Peninsula's diverse terrain is a haven for outdoor enthusiasts, who are drawn to its rugged coastline, dramatic cliffs, and sheltered inlets. Adventure seekers can hike, cycle, or kayak along the coast, uncovering hidden gems and breathtaking vistas at every turn.

The beaches in this part of Ireland are nothing short of spectacular. From the pristine sands of Ballyhiernan Beach to the secluded charm of Portsalon, the Fanad Peninsula treasures some of the most exquisite beaches in Ireland. It's not only the idyllic shores that captivate those visiting – it's the overwhelming sense of tranquility that arises from being enveloped by such extraordinary natural beauty.

In order to reach Fanad Head, the closest airport is in Londonderry/Derry, where you will also find train links from other major cities. You can also rent a car or catch public transport from here out to the peninsula.

Fanad Head is a region of untamed allure and soothing serenity, where ancient tales coexist with contemporary charm. This captivating destination beckons history aficionados, adventure seekers, and solace-searchers alike, promising unforgettable experiences and cherished memories.

For those yearning for a touch of Irish culture, Fanad Head provides a rich tapestry of opportunities. From spirited traditional music sessions in cosy pubs to the lively festivals that animate the area year-round, there is always something to explore and enjoy in this enchanting corner of Ireland. Above all, it is the warmth and hospitality of the locals that make Fanad Head truly unforgettable, as they welcome you with open arms and genuine Irish kindness.

16. Ramelton

Nestled along the banks of the River Lennon, this charming and picturesque village is steeped in history and culture. With its Georgian architecture, vibrant arts scene, and welcoming community, visitors find themselves transported to a bygone era. Stroll the quaint streets, explore the local craft shops, and indulge in delicious Irish cuisine at traditional pubs.

-> From Letterkenny, follow the R245 for 20 minutes to reach the village. Accessible. Dog-friendly.

17. Ballymastocker Beach

Stretching along the picturesque Donegal coast, this award-winning Blue Flag beach is a true hidden gem boasting golden sands, crystal-clear waters, and a serene atmosphere. Surrounded by lush green hills, Ballymastocker Beach offers a tranquil escape from the hustle of everyday life, serving as the perfect setting for swimming, walking, or simply taking in the breathtaking views.

-> To reach Ballymastocker Beach, follow the R246 from Portsalon and turn onto the L11124. Dog-friendly.
///credit.debater.treasuries

18. Great Pollet Sea Arch

Carved by the relentless power of the Atlantic Ocean, this remarkable geological formation captivates visitors with its majestic presence, a true spectacle of Ireland's Wild Atlantic Way. Adventure seekers and nature enthusiasts alike flock to witness the mesmerising arch, a prime spot for photography, hiking, and simply marveling at the sheer beauty of this natural wonder.

-> Take the R245 from Portsalon and turn onto the L2021, following the signs for Pollet. Dog-friendly.
///defraud.relive.rectangles

18 GREAT POLLET SEA ARCH

19. Fanad Head Lighthouse

Perched atop the dramatic cliffs of Donegal, the iconic Fanad Head Lighthouse has guided mariners along Ireland's Wild Atlantic Way since 1817. Its striking white tower, set against the backdrop of the rugged coastline and crashing waves of the Atlantic, is a symbol of resilience and a beacon of hope.

For photography lovers, the landscape surrounding the lighthouse provides a stunning canvas for capturing the raw beauty and dramatic power of nature. The ground floor of the lighthouse and its exhibition area are wheelchair accessible, ensuring that visitors of all abilities can immerse themselves in this unique experience.

-> To reach Fanad Head Lighthouse, take the R245 from Portsalon and follow the signs for Fanad Head. Wheelchair accessible in the ground floor and exhibition area. Dog-friendly. ///repeal.stealthy.dormant

20. Kinny Lough

Nestled amidst the lush green hills of Donegal, the serene Kinny Lough offers an idyllic retreat from the bustling world. This hidden gem along Ireland's Wild Atlantic Way beckons those seeking solace in the heart of nature, providing a picturesque setting for a leisurely walk, a quiet picnic, or a reflective moment of solitude. Surrounded by a tapestry of vibrant flora and a diverse array of birdlife, Kinny Lough is a haven for nature enthusiasts and photographers alike. The tranquil waters of the lough mirror the ever-changing skies above, creating a captivating, ever-shifting landscape that is perfect for those looking to immerse themselves in the beauty of the Irish countryside.

-> Take the R245 from Portsalon and follow the signs for Kinny Lough. Wheelchair accessible. Dog-friendly.

21. Ballyhiernan Beach

This pristine, sandy beach entices visitors to discover its hidden treasures, as the broad expanse of sea and sky creates a backdrop of unparalleled beauty. An interesting fact about the area is that Ballyhiernan Beach is a world-renowned spot for surfers looking to catch the perfect wave.

-> As you head east along Magheradrumman Road, take the second left after Fanad United FC onto the road signposted "to the beach". Dog-friendly. ///justifying.vanity.storeroom

22. Murder Hole Beach

Tucked away along the rugged Donegal coast, the enchanting oasis of Boyeeghter Bay offers a serene retreat for those who venture to its shores. Known as Murder Hole Beach, this hidden gem reveals a pristine stretch of sand, crystal-clear waters, and captivating coves accessible only at low tide. The dramatic cliffs and diverse wildlife further enhance the beach's allure, making it a truly unforgettable destination.

-> Follow the R245 from Milford and watch for signs to Boyeeghter Bay. Park in the car park and walk over the hill to the beach. Roughly a 20 minute walk across soft sand. Dog-friendly. ///behind.starters.handprint

22 MURDER HOLE BEACH (BOYEEGHTER BAY)

23. Tranarossan Bay

Nestled amidst dramatic cliffs and verdant landscapes, the serene waters of Tranarossan Bay create a picture-perfect retreat for visitors seeking solace and natural beauty. The idyllic beach boasts immaculate sandy shores for leisurely strolls and the chance to marvel at magnificent sunsets melting into the expansive horizon. The bay's soothing atmosphere and captivating scenery form a truly unforgettable experience for all who venture there.

-> Start in Milford and take the R245 road, travelling approximately 7 kilometers to Kinnaloughy Crossroads. Turn left onto the L-5461 road, and continue for another 2.5 kilometers until you arrive at the bay. Dog-friendly.
///mindset.owes.unchanging

24. Doe Castle

Set against the backdrop of lush Irish landscapes, this 16th-century fortress serves as a vivid reminder of the region's rich heritage. As one wanders through the ancient stone walls, the castle's storied past comes to life, offering a fascinating glimpse into the lives of the noble families who once called it home.

The picturesque surroundings of Sheephaven Bay amplify the castle's allure, providing an enchanting escape for history buffs and nature lovers alike.

-> From Creeslough, take the R245 road west, then turn right onto L-1202. Continue for 2 km to reach the castle. Dog-friendly. ///revolt.productions.confronts

25. Marble Hill Strand

A picturesque stretch of golden sand in County Donegal, Ireland, awaits those who venture to the idyllic haven known as Marble Hill Strand.

This unspoiled beach, embraced by the Atlantic Ocean, offers an ideal spot for water sports enthusiasts as the beach's gentle waves invite surfers and swimmers to get in the cold water. It is a beautiful beach for a walk along the shore.

-> Follow the R245 road from Letterkenny towards Dunfanaghy. Turn left onto the L1323 road and follow it to the beach's parking area. Dog-friendly.
///deflated.reseal.tasty

25 MARBLE HILL STRAND

26. Tory island
A mystical gem off the coast of County Donegal, Ireland, the remote Tory Island enchants visitors with its rich history, vibrant culture, and stunning landscapes. Home to a close-knit community of artists and musicians, the island's creative spirit flourishes amidst the breathtaking cliffs, lighthouses, and ancient monastic ruins. Tory Island's allure lies in its authentic Irish charm, where visitors become part of the tapestry of life in this captivating haven.

-> *Take a ferry from either Bunbeg or Magheroarty in County Donegal. It is important to check the ferry schedules, as they vary depending on weather conditions and time of year. No explicit mention of wheelchair accessibility, so it is best to inquire with individual establishments and attractions. Dog-friendly. ///stripped.auctions.workspace*

27. Bloody Foreland
At the edge of Ireland's rugged northwest coast lies a striking headland steeped in history and folklore. Bloody Foreland, so named for the reddish hue of its granite rocks, captivates visitors with breathtaking views of the Atlantic Ocean and the surrounding landscape.

As the sun sets, the rocks' crimson glow intensifies, evoking a sense of awe and wonder. This natural marvel offers a unique opportunity to immerse oneself in the beauty and mystery of the Emerald Isle.

-> *Start in Gweedore, County Donegal, and follow the R257 northwest towards Brinlack. Takes approximately 20 minutes by car. Dog-friendly. ///unblinking.gangs.bazaars*

28 BUNBEG

28. Bunbeg

Cradled along the stunning Donegal coastline, a tranquil village entices visitors with its serene beauty and warmth. With inviting sandy beaches, crystalline waters, and traditional Irish pubs, Bunbeg provides a picturesque retreat for those seeking both adventure and relaxation. Embracing the breathtaking Wild Atlantic Way, this idyllic destination blends unspoiled natural landscapes, genuine hospitality, and a rich Gaelic heritage to create an unforgettable experience.

-> Travel west from Letterkenny, County Donegal, on the N56 for approximately 50 minutes, then turn right onto the R258 at Meenacuing Bridge. Wheelchair accessible. Dog-friendly.

29. Carrickfin Beach

A hidden gem along the stunning Donegal coastline, this breathtaking sanctuary of golden sands and turquoise waters beckons you to relax and rejuvenate.

Carrickfin Beach offers a serene escape from the chaos of everyday life, surrounded by awe-inspiring landscapes that leave you feeling at one with nature. The captivating beauty and peaceful atmosphere make it an unforgettable destination for all who visit.

-> Travel northwest from Dungloe in County Donegal, following the R259 road towards the coast. The beach is well-signposted and easily reachable by car. Wheelchair accessible. Dog-friendly. ///consisting.chunks.belonged

29 CARRICKFIN BEACH

28 BUNBEG

Where to Eat
in Fanad Head

Leo's Tavern
In the picturesque village of Meenaleck, Leo's Tavern is a cherished Irish pub and music venue with a rich history. It is renowned as the birthplace of Clannad, the iconic Irish band. Visitors can enjoy traditional Irish music, hearty cuisine, and soak up the warm and welcoming atmosphere.
-> F92 F29T. Wheelchair Accessible. ///impressions.biding.surplus

Batch Donegal
Batch is a trendy restaurant that blends modern cuisine with the warmth of Irish hospitality. With a focus on locally sourced ingredients, Batch offers a culinary experience that highlights the flavours and traditions of the region.
-> F92 APY. ///antenna.pinches.postmodern

The Rusty Oven - Pizzeria
Step into this cosy pizzeria and be greeted by the delightful scent of freshly baked dough. The Rusty Oven prides itself on crafting authentic, wood-fired pizzas using only the finest ingredients. Whether you're a fan of classic Margherita or adventurous toppings, the menu offers something for everyone.
-> F92 A8RH. Wheelchair Accessible. ///defectors.defers.lightless

The Shack - Artisan Coffee & Ice Cream
A charming coffee shop and ice cream parlour that embraces the art of handcrafted treats. From expertly brewed coffees to creamy, homemade ice cream flavours, The Shack offers a delightful indulgence for those seeking a flavourful experience in a cosy, artistic setting.
-> F92 CK29. Wheelchair Accessible. Dog-friendly. ///clangs.duplex.beekeepers

Crêpe Hatch
Savour the flavours of France with Crêpe Hatch, a charming crêperie nestled at the tranquil beach of Rosapenna. Indulge in the handcrafted, sweet and savoury crêpes that are sure to delight your taste buds.
-> F92 X73F. Wheelchair Accessible. Dog-friendly. ///mildest.instead.carnations

Fisk Seafood Bar Downings
Discover the taste of the sea at Fisk Seafood Bar in Downings. This charming seafood bar offers a variety of fresh, locally sourced seafood dishes that will satisfy any seafood lover's cravings. Sitting right by the harbour, seafood here does not get much fresher that this.
-> F92 XR53. ///precarious.buyers.heartbreak

Where to Stay
in Fanad Head

Hotels
- Castle Grove Country House (Dog-friendly)
- Mount Errigal Hotel
- Mulroy Woods Hotel (Wheelchair Accessible. Dog-friendly)
- Shandon Hotel & Spa (Wheelchair Accessible)

Self-Catering Apartments
- Corcreggan Mill (Dog-friendly)
- Bunbeg Lodge (Wheelchair Accessible. Dog-friendly)
- Song House

Campsites

Quiet Moments Camping Site
This tranquil and secluded campsite offers a peaceful escape from the hustle and bustle of everyday life. Enjoy the serene atmosphere and scenic surroundings in a variety of accommodations, including tent pitches and caravan sites, while taking advantage of the many facilities provided for guests.
-> F92 W065. Dog-friendly. ///ankles.dipper.baffles

Caseys Caravan & Camping Park, Donegal
This family-friendly park offers a range of camping options, from spacious pitches for tents to caravan sites with all the necessary amenities. Guests can enjoy stunning views of the Atlantic Ocean while taking advantage of the park's many facilities, including a children's playground, on-site shop, and electric hookup points.
->F92 H7WK. Dog-friendly. ///class.venture.sprung

Sleepy Hollows
With a variety of camping options available, from tent pitches to motorhome sites, you can choose the perfect accommodation for your needs. Enjoy the stunning views, explore the nearby hiking trails, or simply relax by the campfire and soak in the serenity of Sleepy Hollows.
-> F92 HK73. Dog-friendly. ///noting.raving.magician

Roadtrip Essentials
in Fanad Head

Food Shops
- Aldi, Letterkenny
- Tesco, Letterkenny
- Creeslough Supermarket
- Centra, Dunfanaghy
- McGinley's Supermarket Falcarragh
- Spar, Derrybeg

Water Points and CDP
- St Eunan's GAA Club (Water & CDP)
- Falcarragh Car Park (Water & CDP)
- Mgheroarty Pier (Water & CDP)
- Derrybeg Spar (Water only)
- Gortahork Spar (Water only)
- Dunfanaghy Beach Car Park (Water only)
- Rathmullan Pier Car Park (Water only)

Electric Vehicle Charging Points
- "EVBox Charging Station, gTeic Goath Dohair ///rebounding.classical.elbowing
- EBS Charging Station, Strand Rd ///relit.architect.fever
- ChargePoint Charging Station, Rosapenna Hotel ///diluting.compressed.monthly
- GOcharge Charging Station: Kinnegar, Rathmullan ///dirt.entries.resonating"

21 BALLYHIERNAN BEACH

23 TRANAROSSAN BAY

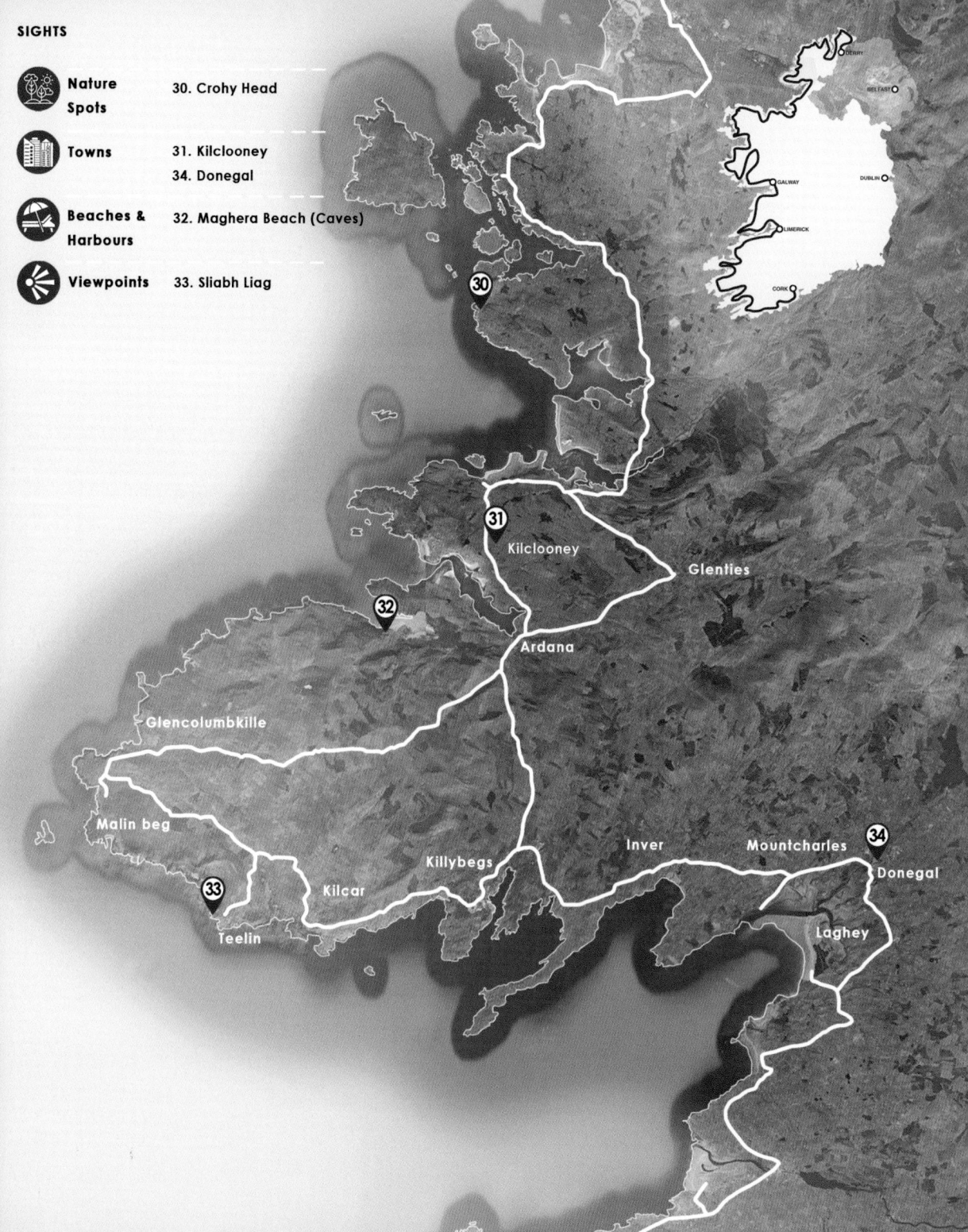

Sliabh Liag Coast

Nestled in the charming northwestern region of the Wild Atlantic Way, the Slieve League area in Ireland is an incredible destination where nature's magnificence reigns supreme. Rich in folklore and steeped in cultural heritage, the Sliabh Liag (Slieve League) area invites visitors to immerse themselves in Ireland's fascinating history through its ancient relics, crumbling fortresses, and age-old churches.

Beyond its historical charm, the Slieve League area features some of Ireland's most breathtaking landscapes. From the awe-inspiring Sliabh Liag Cliffs, which stand among the tallest sea cliffs in Europe, to the tranquil waters of Teelin Bay, the region's beauty is truly unrivalled.

The Sliabh Liag area's diverse terrain creates a sanctuary for outdoor enthusiasts, attracted by its dramatic coastline, towering cliffs, and hidden coves. Adventurers can hike, cycle, or kayak along the shore, discovering remarkable treasures and stunning panoramas at every bend.

Naturally, the beaches are nothing short of extraordinary. From the unspoiled sands of Silver Strand to the secluded charm of Muckross, the Sliabh Liag area treasures some of the most exceptional beaches in Ireland. The charm lies not only in the picturesque shores but also in the overwhelming sense of serenity that emanates from being surrounded by such remarkable natural beauty.

In order to reach Sliabh Liag, the closest airport is in Donegal. You can reach this area easily by public transport, transiting to Donegal by train and then changing to the local bus service. You can also rent a car from here and drive out to the coastline.

The Sliabh Liag area is a region of vivid contrasts - a domain of wild beauty and calming tranquillity, where ancient legends harmoniously coexist with modern allure. This mesmerising destination entices history enthusiasts, adventure lovers, and tranquillity-seekers alike, delivering unforgettable experiences and treasured memories.

As you traverse the winding roads leading to the towering cliffs, a sense of awe washes over you, accentuated by the expanse of the Atlantic Ocean stretching out as far as the eye can see. The crisp sea air fills your lungs and the rhythmic crashing of waves against the cliff base becomes the soundtrack to your journey.

For those craving a touch of Irish culture, the Sliabh Liag area offers a rich array of opportunities. From spirited traditional music sessions in welcoming pubs to the vibrant festivals that enliven the region throughout the year, there is always something to discover and relish in this magical corner of Ireland.

30. Crohy Head
Perched on the edge of the rugged Irish coastline, a dramatic vista awaits those who venture to this untamed location. Crohy Head, with its towering sea arch and captivating views, offers an exhilarating experience for nature lovers and adventurers alike.

The raw beauty of its surroundings serves as a reminder of the indomitable force of the elements, leaving visitors in awe of the sheer power and majesty of the landscape.

-> Start in the village of Maghery and follow the local road R230 towards the coast. Then, take the L1013 road, which will lead you to Crohy Head. Dog-friendly. ///rituals.pining.dragonfly

30 CROHY HEAD

31. Kilclooney

Steeped in history and enveloped in natural beauty, the small Irish town of Kilclooney offers a glimpse into the country's rich past. Renowned for the iconic Kilclooney Dolmen, this ancient portal tomb serves as a testament to Ireland's rich neolithic heritage.

The picturesque landscape surrounding Kilclooney invites visitors to explore its rolling hills, lush valleys, and timeless charm, creating an unforgettable experience for all who wander there.

-> Travel from Ardara in County Donegal along the N56 road. Turn left onto the Loughros Point Road (R261), and continue until you reach the Kilclooney Dolmen signpost. Dog-friendy. ///benign.playable.arming

32 MAGHERA BEACH

32. Maghera Beach

With its pristine white sands and crystal-clear turquoise waters, this hidden gem transports visitors to a tranquil paradise. Nestled along the scenic coastline, Maghera Beach offers a picturesque setting for relaxation or a walk on along the sand. Surrounded by towering cliffs and vibrant flora, the beach provides a serene escape from the bustling city life.

Those seeking adventure can explore the fascinating caves that can be found along the cliffs or embark on a scenic coastal hike. Maghera Beach can be a dangerous place to swim due to strong rip tides and it is not advised to swim at this beach.

-> Maghera Beach can be reached by taking the N56 road from Donegal town and then following the signs to the beach. Dog-friendly. ///patrolled.wildly.bargains

33. Sliabh Liag

Majestic and strong, the towering cliffs of Sliabh Liag stand sentinel along the breathtaking Wild Atlantic Way. Among the highest sea cliffs in Europe, sitting at a total of 601m, these natural wonders offer sweeping panoramas of the untamed Irish coastline, where land and sea exist in perfect harmony.

You can either walk to the viewpoint from the car park that sits a 1.5km walk from the platform, or alternatively, you can enjoy a scenic bus ride from the nearby visitor centre. This option allows you to hear stories about the local area from the tour guide as you soak up the stunning surroundings on the drive to the top of the hill.

-> *From Killybegs follow the R263 road heading through Carrick to the Sliabh Liag Cliffs Centre. From there, you can walk or pay a small fee for a convenient bus ride. Wheelchair accessible. Dog-friendly. ///gardens.affair. upstanding*

33 SLIABH LIAG

34. Donegal

Immersed in the splendour of Ireland's northwestern landscape, the quaint town of Donegal offers a delightful escape from the ordinary. Bustling streets, inviting shops, and lively pubs set the stage for a journey into the heart of Irish history and culture. The majestic Donegal Castle, a 15th-century marvel, stands as a testament to the town's storied past.

Meanwhile, the picturesque River Eske provides a serene backdrop for leisurely strolls and quiet reflection. The bustling Diamond, a central gathering place, serves as a melting pot where locals and visitors come together to share stories and create new memories.

34 DONEGAL

-> *Fly into Donegal Airport and rent a car or take a bus to explore the county. Alternatively, do the same in Belfast and drive northwest toward Donegal. Wheelchair accessible. Dog-friendly. ///found.weekends.zone*

Where to Eat
on the Sliabh Liag Coast

Chill the Beans
A cute coffee van that can be found just a stones throw from the hugely popular swimming port of Illanamarve Harbour. This tiny van is a very welcome sight as a place to enjoy a hot drink after a refreshing dip in the North Atlantic.

-> F94 YT54. Wheelchair Accessible. Dog-friendly. ///conjunction.brokered.carnivorous

The Lobster Pot
Specialising in fresh seafood caught daily, The Lobster Pot offers a delectable menu featuring dishes such as lobster bisque, crab claws, and pan-fried hake. With its stunning coastal views and warm, inviting ambiance, this restaurant provides a memorable dining experience.

-> F94 HD91. ///drastic.frost.reversals

The Rusty Mackerel
Rated as the No.1 restaurant in the area, the Rusty Mackerel offers a unique dining experience with its cozy and rustic atmosphere. Enjoy delicious locally sourced food while soaking in the stunning views of the surrounding mountains and valleys.

-> F94 VP99. Wheelchair Accessible. Dog-friendly. ///hippos.moments.trees

The Harbour Restaurant
A charming dining spot offering delicious seafood, including, locally sourced ingredients, traditional Irish cuisine, and refreshing drinks. Its waterfront location provides stunning views, making it the perfect place for a delightful dining experience.

-> F94 R660. ///tablet.aura.them

Blueberry Tea Room and Restaurant
A popular and charming tea room offering a delightful selection of teas, homemade cakes, and scones. Visitors can enjoy a cosy and inviting atmosphere while indulging in delicious treats and enjoying the picturesque town of Donegal.

-> F94 AH75. ///wrong.skis.points

Salthill Cabin
Salthill Cabin, situated at Mountcharles Pier, offers breathtaking views of the pier and beach. This charming cabin is ideal for those with small children, with its onsite petting zoo, full of rescued animals of all shapes and sizes. From owls to goats, peacocks and a lot of chickens, this coffee cabin has it all.

-> F94 DW73. Wheelchair Accessible. Dog-friendly. ///influence.carpentry.recycling

Where to Stay
on the Sliabh Liag Coast

Hotels
- Arranmore Glamping (Dog-friendly)
- Waterfront Hotel (Wheelchair Accessible)
- Woodhill House (Wheelchair Accessible)
- Tara Hotel
- Malinbeg Hostel
- Slieve League Inn
- The Abbey Hotel (Wheelchair Accessible)

Self-Catering Apartments
- Dungloe Rooms and Apartments (Wheelchair Accessible. Dog-friendly)
- Drumbarron Cottage
- Trident Holiday Homes (Wheelchair Accessible. Dog-friendly)
- The Loft
- Corrakille House

Campsites

Tramore Beach Caravan and Camping Park
Located near Tramore Beach, this park offers a variety of accommodation options for camping and caravanning. Whether you prefer to camp under the stars or stay in a caravan, this park has you covered.
-> *F94 RW66. Dog-friendly. ///regionally.lander.circulates*

Sliabh Liag Camping
A family-run campsite located on the edge of Ireland's beautiful Wild Atlantic Way, providing guests with the perfect base for exploring the scenic sights of Donegal. The campsite offers a range of facilities, including electric hookups, showers, and a campers' kitchen.
-> *F94 X2XV. Dog-friendly. ///subtitled.flamed.publication*

Dungloe Caravan Park
A convenient base for campers to explore the local area, including nearby beaches and picturesque landscapes. The park offers a range of amenities, including electric hookups, showers, and a campers' kitchen. Its central location and friendly atmosphere make it a popular choice for visitors to Dungloe.
-> *F94 YY28. Dog-friendly. ///avenge.shelter.souvenir*

Roadtrip Essentials
on the Sliabh Liag Coast

Food Shops
- Aldi, Dungloe
- Lidl, Dungloe
- Costcutter, Drumnasillagh
- Darnell's Spar Portnoo
- Centra, Kilcar
- Aldi, Donegal
- Lidl, Donegal

Water Points and CDP
- Maghery Service Area (Water & CDP)
- Spierstown Campsite (Water & CDP)
- Crolly Service Station (Water only)
- Dungloe Public Toilets (Water only)
- Ardara Car Park (Water only)
- Bruckless Service Station (Water only)
- Mountcharles Pier (Water only)

Electric Vehicle Charging Points
- EVBox Charging Station, Donegal Airport ///server.debating.contesting
- ESB Charging Station, Lower Main Street, Dunglow ///attentive.conjuring.sampled
- ecars Charge Point Charging Station, Mill Road ///prevailed.reserving.spruce
- ESB Charging Station, Shore Road, Cashelcummin ///flights.supports.overslept
- Tesla Destination Charger, The Mullins ///safe.vehicle.kinks
- ecars Charge Point: Quay St ///breath.prepares.fanfare
- EasyGo Charging Station Drumlonagher ///connects.labels.jetted

SIGHTS

- **Beaches & Harbours** — 35. Murvagh Beach
- **Nature Spots** — 36. Tullan Strand (Fairy Bridge)
  41. Mullaghmore Head - Bishops Pool
- **Towns** — 37. Raghly
- **Mountains** — 38. Benbulbin
- **Waterfalls** — 39. Glencar Waterfall
- **Castles & Historical Sights** — 40. Sligo Abbey

Donegal Bay and Sligo

As the rugged coastline of Donegal Bay stretches before you, the raw power of the Atlantic Ocean collides with the wild, untamed beauty of the shore, leaving you in awe of nature's sheer force. The salty breeze whispers ancient tales, as the tranquil shores of St. John's Point Lighthouse offer solace amidst the vast expanse.

In the distance, the majestic silhouette of Benbulben Mountain looms over the enchanting town of Sligo, inspiring poets and painters alike. Wander through the hauntingly beautiful ruins of Sligo Abbey, where the echoes of a bygone era resonate with the hallowed walls. The verdant landscape of Yeats Country envelops you in a warm embrace, transporting you to a realm where words and nature intertwine seamlessly. Stand on the windswept shores of Rosses Point, as the waves crash against the rocks, and let the ethereal beauty of the region wash over you.

The Donegal Bay and Sligo region is an area not to be missed on your Wild Atlantic Way road trip.

In order to reach this region, the closest airport is in Sligo. You can reach this area easily by public transport, transiting to Sligo by train and then changing to the local bus service. You can also rent a car from here and drive out to the coastline.

Donegal Bay and Sligo form a picturesque region in the northwestern part of Ireland, boasting a unique blend of stunning landscapes, rich history, and cultural heritage. Donegal Bay, with its 113kms of coastline, is home to several charming towns and fishing villages, such as Killybegs and Bundoran. The bay is also a hub for aquatic activities, including sailing, surfing, and angling, attracting enthusiasts from around the world.

Sligo, known as Yeats Country, has strong connections to the renowned Irish poet W.B. Yeats, who drew inspiration from the area's natural beauty. The town of Sligo is home to the famous Sligo Abbey, a 13th-century Dominican monastery with beautiful Gothic and Renaissance architectural features. The dramatic limestone formation of Benbulben Mountain dominates the landscape and offers numerous walking trails for hikers to explore.

Visitors to Donegal Bay and Sligo can enjoy a wide range of outdoor activities, such as hiking, golfing, and horse riding, while also immersing themselves in the local arts and crafts scene, which showcases traditional Irish craftsmanship. With its blend of natural beauty, historical sites, and cultural attractions, the region of Donegal Bay and Sligo is an enriching destination for travellers seeking an authentic Irish experience.

35. Murvagh Beach

A peaceful haven awaits you along the picturesque coastline of Donegal Bay, where the enchanting Murvagh Beach offers an idyllic retreat. This expansive stretch of fine golden sand, backed by magnificent dunes, provides a tranquil respite for those seeking peace and quiet amidst nature's beauty.

Known for its excellent water quality, the beach is perfect for swimming, sunbathing, and building sandcastles. As the sun sets, a mesmerising display of colours paints the sky, leaving an indelible impression on all who experience it.

-> Take the N15 from Donegal Town towards Ballyshannon, and turn left onto the L2165 at the Murvagh signpost. Continue for 4 kms until you reach the beach's car park. Dog-friendly. ///helpful.marvel.solutions

35 MURVAGH BEACH

36 TULLAN STRAND (FAIRY BRIDGE)

36. Tullan Strand

Embraced by the Wild Atlantic Way's rugged beauty, the breathtaking Tullan Strand captivates visitors with its golden sands and undulating dunes. Renowned for its excellent surf conditions, this expansive, crescent-shaped beach is a haven for watersports enthusiasts.

Adding a touch of enchantment to this picturesque beach, the nearby Fairy Bridge, a charming natural arch formed by centuries of coastal erosion, invites curiosity and wonder.

-> Follow the N15 from Ballyshannon towards Bundoran and turn left onto the R267. Continue along this road until you reach the Tullan Strand Road and the beach car park. Wheelchair accessible. Dog-friendly. ///zest.fatter.childbirth

37. Raghly

Nestled in the heart of County Sligo, the tranquil seaside village of Raghly boasts panoramic views of the Atlantic Ocean and the iconic Benbulben mountain. This coastal gem offers visitors a serene escape, where the gentle rustle of sea breeze mingles with the melodic calls of native birds.

The picturesque harbour, a focal point of the village, provides a peaceful ambiance for leisurely strolls or quiet moments of reflection. Raghly's unspoiled charm and natural beauty make it an idyllic destination for those seeking reprieve from the bustle of everyday life.

-> *Travel along the N15 from Sligo Town towards Grange, and turn right onto the L3202 at the Drumcliff roundabout. Continue for 9 kms until you arrive in the village. Wheelchair accessibility. Dog-friendly. ///tequila.resetting.buddies*

38. Benbulbin

Rising majestically from the surrounding landscape, the iconic flat-topped limestone formation in County Sligo, captivates visitors with its breathtaking beauty and unique geological features. Known as Benbulbin, this striking table mountain is steeped in Irish folklore.

Hikers and nature lovers alike are drawn to the area to explore its scenic trails, abundant flora, and fauna, and to soak in the stunning views from its summit. A visit to this enchanting natural wonder promises an unforgettable experience for all who venture to its slopes.

-> *Take the N15 road from Sligo Town towards Bundoran. Turn right onto the R278 road and continue for approximately 8 km. Turn left onto a minor road and follow it for about 2 km. ///definite.hallways.introduces*

38 BENBULBIN

41 MULLAGHMORE HEAD (BISHOPS POOL)

40 SLIGO ABBEY

39. Glencar Waterfall

Tucked away in the serene and lush Glencar Valley of County Leitrim, Ireland, lies a mesmerising cascade of water that has inspired poets and enchanted visitors for generations. This enchanting natural wonder, Glencar Waterfall, plummets gracefully from a height of 50 feet into a tranquil pool below, surrounded by verdant foliage and rocky outcrops.

The soothing sounds of the waterfall, combined with the captivating beauty of the area, create a truly magical atmosphere. A visit to this hidden gem offers a rejuvenating experience and a chance to reconnect with nature's splendour.

-> Take the N16 road towards Manorhamilton. Turn right onto R286 and continue for 8 km. Turn left onto the L1013 road and follow it for 1.5 km until you reach the waterfall car park. Dog-friendly. ///rummage.posts.copied

40. Sligo Abbey

Steeped in history and shrouded in mystery, the hauntingly beautiful ruins of a 13th-century Dominican friary beckon visitors to explore their storied past. Located in the heart of Sligo Town, Ireland, Sligo Abbey has withstood the test of time, bearing witness to turbulent events and changing hands throughout the centuries. Its intricate carvings, gothic architecture, and atmospheric setting provide a fascinating glimpse into medieval monastic life.

As you wander through the hallowed grounds, let your imagination transport you back in time and experience the echoes of a bygone era.

-> Located on Abbey Street, just a short walk from the town's central O'Connell Street. Wheelchair Accessible. ///bikers.marker.referral

41. Mullaghmore Head - Bishops Pool

A hidden oasis awaits discovery along the Wild Atlantic Way in County Sligo, Ireland. The Mullaghmore Head Bishops Pool, nestled between rugged cliffs and the azure waters of the Atlantic Ocean, offers visitors a unique and invigorating experience. This natural seawater pool, carved into the rocky shoreline, provides a refreshing respite amongst the stunning coastline of Mullaghmore Head. The awe-inspiring views and enchanting atmosphere make it an idyllic spot for a tranquil swim or a leisurely picnic. Immerse yourself in the captivating beauty of this coastal haven and create lasting memories.

-> *Follow the N15 road towards Bundoran. Turn right onto R279 and continue for 8 km until you reach the village of Mullaghmore. From the village, follow the signs for Mullaghmore Head and Bishops Pool. Dog-friendly.*
///text.stops.etched

Where to Eat
in Donegal Bay and Sligo

Rambling House Bar & Restaurant
Known for its warm hospitality and traditional Irish atmosphere, it offers a delightful dining experience with a menu showcasing a fusion of local and international cuisine. The bar is a popular spot for enjoying live music, creating a lively and welcoming atmosphere for locals and visitors alike.

-> F94 Y048. Wheelchair accessible. Dog-friendly. ///endowments.cascading.sample

Henrys Bar & Restaurant
With a lively atmosphere and friendly staff, it offers a unique dining and drinking experience. The menu features a variety of mouthwatering dishes, including traditional Irish fare and contemporary favourites. Whether you're looking for a relaxing meal or a fun night out, Henry's is the perfect spot to enjoy good food and good company.

-> F91 PF96. Wheelchair accessible. ///rigid.covert.raft

Shannon's Corner Restaurant
This quaint eatery offers a cosy atmosphere and serves up delicious meals made with locally sourced ingredients. From traditional Irish dishes to international flavours, Shannon's Corner pleases the palate of both locals and tourists, making it a must-visit dining destination in the area.

-> F94 NF83. Wheelchair accessible. ///stigmas.devote.misconduct

Flipside
Flipside is a trendy café and restaurant located in the heart of Sligo town. The menu offers a modern take on classic dishes with a focus on fresh, locally sourced ingredients. The atmosphere is laid-back, perfect for catching up with friends over a cup of coffee, or enjoying a leisurely brunch on the weekend.

-> F91 XPX9. ///deeper.tank.magnets

Eithna's By the Sea Restaurant
Specialising in fresh seafood, this charming restaurant offers a menu that highlights the best of local flavours and traditional recipes. With stunning views of the sea and a warm, welcoming ambiance, Eithna's is a favorite among seafood enthusiasts and those seeking a memorable dining experience.

-> F91 FF24. Wheelchair accessible. ///marketplace.toil.diameters

Coach Lane Restaurant at Donaghy's Bar
Situated within the historic walls of Donaghy's Bar, this restaurant offers a unique dining experience with a warm and welcoming atmosphere. From hearty pub classics to more sophisticated gourmet options, Coach Lane Restaurant caters to all tastes and preferences.

-> F91 RR23. ///honestly.marginal.refers

Where to Stay
in Donegal Bay and Sligo

Hotels
- Rossmore Farmhouse B&B
- The Sandhouse Hotel (Wheelchair Accessible)
- Coolmore Manor House & Siraxta Horses
- Holland House B&B (Wheelchair Accessible)
- Creevy Pier Hotel
- Heron's Cove (Wheelchair Accessible)

Self-Catering Apartments
- The Honeycomb Chalet
- Sunset Lodge
- Cavangarden Court (Wheelchair Accessible)
- Rossnowlagh Waves Lodge
- Surfers Delight Holiday Home

Campsites

Lakeside Caravan & Camping
Lakeside Caravan and Camping is a four-star rated park located on the banks of Assaroe Lake in Sligo. It's a perfect holiday destination to explore the Wild Atlantic Way or use as a base. With modern amenities and serene atmosphere, the park provides an unforgettable camping experience.
-> F94 KX53. ///payphone.largely.lacked

Boortree Touring Rossnowlagh
A perfect destination to explore the North West of Ireland. It provides a convenient base for visitors to experience the beauty of the area. The website lacks specific details on facilities and amenities, but the location offers potential for outdoor activities and sightseeing.
-> F94 W64W. Dog-friendly.
///squabble.boast.swiftly

Greenlands Caravan & Camping
A spectacular coastal destination in County Sligo that offers spacious camping sites and cosy cabins. With its stunning views of the sea and surrounding countryside, it's the ideal location for a peaceful retreat. The park is equipped with modern facilities, including a playground and laundry, ensuring guests make the most of their stay.
-> F91 Y974. ///enveloped.utility.objective

36 TULLAN STRAND (FAIRY BRIDGE)

Roadtrip Essentials
in Donegal Bay and Sligo

Food Shops
- Spar, Kernan's
- Centra, Ballyshannon
- Lidl, Bundorran
- Spar, Kinlough
- Lidl, Sligo
- Aldi, Sligo

Water Points
- Enniskellen Service Station (Water only)
- Bundoran Service Station (Water only)
- Tullaghan Service Station (Water only)
- Mullaghmore Harbour (Water only)
- Grange Service Station (Water only)
- Clooneen Service Station (Water only)
- Today's Express Sligo (Water only)

Electric Vehicle Charging Points
- ESB Charging Station, Laghy ///squashed.opener.conquered
- Tesla Destination Charger, 8 Bayview Tar ///consumed.frontline.endowments
- ecars Charge Point: N15 Drumcliffe Nort ///graphs.lampshade.votes
- LiFe Charging Station, Ash Ln ///sardine.treble.shady
- ESB Charging Station. Texaco, Grange ///protesting.february.voluptuous
- Monta Charging Station Swan Poin ///commands.normal.cheeses
- ESB Charging Station, Abbeyquarter North ///parties.fears.slope

36 TULLAN STRAND (FAIRY BRIDGE)

SIGHTS

 Castles & Historical Sights
42. Rosserk Friary
45. Ceide Fields

 Beaches & Harbours
43. Carrowmore Beach

 Viewpoints
44. Downpatrick Head
46. Benwee Head

Erris

The enchanting charm of Erris on the wild west coast of Ireland invites you to explore its untamed beauty and rich cultural heritage. There are stories of ancient legends that lie throughout the historical sights, while the rugged cliffs and pristine beaches evoke a sense of awe and wonder. In the heart of this captivating landscape, the vibrant colours of the boglands and rolling hills paint a vivid picture of Ireland's natural beauty.

Venture into the charming villages and embrace the warmth of Irish hospitality, as the rich history of Erris engulfs you. The region's breathtaking scenery has inspired countless artists and dreamers, leaving an indelible impression on all who wander its intriguing paths. As you stroll along the windswept shores, the crashing waves of the Atlantic Ocean serve as a powerful reminder of nature's sheer force and timeless beauty.

Erris is a symphony of raw emotion and breathtaking wilderness waiting to be explored on the west coast of Ireland.

In order to reach this region, the closest airport is in Sligo. You can reach this area easily by public transport, transiting to Sligo by train and then changing to the local bus service. You can also rent a car from here and drive out to the coastline.

Erris, a captivating region on the wild west coast of Ireland, offers an impressive fusion of breathtaking landscapes, fascinating history, and vibrant cultural heritage. This charming area treasures miles of rugged coastline, pristine beaches, and rolling hills, providing an idyllic setting for picturesque towns and villages that dot the landscape. Erris is also a haven for outdoor enthusiasts, with activities such as hiking, cycling, and water sports drawing visitors from far and wide.

The region's rich cultural heritage is woven with tales of ancient legends and traditions, which continue to inspire artists and poets alike. At the heart of Erris, the charming villages exude warmth and hospitality, inviting visitors to explore the local arts and crafts scene, showcasing the finest examples of traditional Irish craftsmanship.

42. Rosserk Friary

Amidst the verdant landscape of County Mayo, a 15th-century Franciscan Friary stands as a testament to Ireland's rich monastic tradition. Rosserk Friary, adorned with intricate stone carvings and remarkably preserved architecture, invites visitors to step back in time and explore the lives of the friars who once called this sacred place home. As you wander through the hallowed grounds, the serenity of the surrounding landscape and the echoes of history create an atmosphere of reverence and reflection.

-> Follow the N26 road from Ballina towards Foxford. Turn left onto L1202 road and continue for 3 km until you reach the friary. Dog-friendly. Wheelchair Accessible. ///redevelop.gearbox.objective

43. Carrowmore Beach

A hidden gem on the rugged west coast of Ireland, this pristine stretch of sand and pebbles beckons visitors with its stunning vistas and tranquil atmosphere. Carrowmore Beach, nestled between the dramatic cliffs and the azure waters of the Atlantic Ocean, offers a serene escape from the hustle and bustle of daily life. The breathtaking views and invigorating sea air make it an idyllic spot for a leisurely stroll or a refreshing swim, creating lasting memories amidst the beauty of nature.

-> Follow the N59 road from Westport towards Leenane. Turn left onto the L1820 road and continue for 5 km until you reach the beach. Dog-friendly. ///denote.saucer.anchor

42 ROSSERK FRIARY

44. Downpatrick Head

A majestic promontory rises from the rugged coastline of County Mayo, offering a breathtaking panorama of the wild Atlantic Ocean. Downpatrick Head, steeped in both history and folklore, captivates visitors with its magnificent sea stack, Dún Briste, and the remnants of a church founded by St. Patrick.

As the waves relentlessly batter the towering cliffs, the site's ancient heritage and natural beauty are unforgettable.

-> Follow the R314 road from Ballina towards Ballycastle. Turn right onto the L1203 road and continue for 5 km until you arrive. Wheelchair accessible.
///flicked.venoms.loping

43 CARROWMORE BEACH

45 CEIDE FIELDS

45. Ceide Fields

A testament to the resilience of human ingenuity, an ancient landscape lies hidden beneath the wild blanket bogs of North Mayo. This treasure, known as Céide Fields, holds the secrets of a 6,000-year-old Neolithic farming community, offering a fascinating glimpse into the lives of our ancestors.

As you explore the sprawling expanse of stone walls and megalithic tombs, the whispers of the past intertwine with the rugged beauty of the present, creating a truly immersive experience that transcends the boundaries of time.

-> Follow the N59 road from Ballina towards Ballycastle. Turn right onto the R314 road and continue for 11 km, then turn left onto the L1204 road and follow the signs to the visitor centre. Wheelchair accessible.
///culture.backdrops.serenade

46. Benwee Head

Breathtaking panoramas and untamed beauty await visitors at the dramatic coastal cliffs of County Mayo. Benwee Head, standing tall above the wild Atlantic Ocean, offers unparalleled views of the surrounding landscape and the distant Stags of Broadhaven.

As the wind blows through the heather and the gulls cry overhead, the beautiful views and rugged charm of this remote location create a truly unforgettable experience in this part of Ireland's wild west coast.

-> Follow the R313 road from Belmullet towards Portacloy. Turn left onto the L1205 road and continue for 7 km until you arrive. ///crater.forgive.yielded

Where to Eat
in Erris

Gilroy's Bar and Áit Eile Restaurant
Gilroy's Bar & Ait Eile Restaurant in Enniscrone, County Sligo, is highly recommended for its food, service, and atmosphere. Reviewers praised the seafood dishes such as roasted hake, seafood linguine, and avocado and crab salad.
-> F26 D596. Wheelchair Accessible.
///relentless.proud.daft

Mary's Bakery
From the friendly and welcoming staff, including the owner Mary and her daughter Geraldine, to the mouthwatering desserts and homemade stew, everything at Mary's exceeds expectations. The lemon meringue and lemon cheesecake are also must try items.
-> F26 X5N3. Wheelchair Accessible.
///undamaged.plucky.join

The Old Post Office Coffee Shop & Bakery
Praised for its great coffee, friendly staff, clean facilities, and bright decor, customers highly recommend the food, cakes, and coffee, and appreciate the warm and welcoming atmosphere of this charming cafe.
-> F26 RH51. Wheelchair Accessible.
///inhaler.gateway.knockoffs

Dillons Bar & Restaurant
Dillons Bar & Restaurant in Ballina, County Mayo, Western Ireland, offers exceptional cuisine and a cosy atmosphere. The menu boasts a wide selection of dishes, with generous portions that satisfy any appetite. The friendly and attentive staff ensures a pleasant dining experience.
-> F26 H2X0. Wheelchair Accessible. ///wholesaler.clambered.dimes

Sizzlers Restaurant
With excellent food, great value for money, and a welcoming atmosphere, Sizzler's is a dining experience you won't want to miss. The friendly staff and varied menu, including gluten-free options, cater to a wide range of tastes. Additionally, the restaurant's cosy and pristine interior adds to the overall appeal.
-> H62 VX82. ///stones.resolves.sleepiness

Poacher Restaurant
The menu at the Poacher is described as creative and offers a variety of options, including vegan and vegetarian choices. With a comfortable and relaxed atmosphere, making it a great place for a family dinner or a special occasion.
-> F26 Y5D1. ///belong.dependents.objects

42 ROSSERK FRIARY

Where to Stay
in Erris

Hotels
- Ice House Hotel (Wheelchair Accessible)
- Heyday Ballina
- The Merry Monk (Dog-friendly)
- The Acres Killala
- Ceide Glamping (Wheelchair Accessible)
- Kilcommon Lodge Holiday Hostel

Self-Catering Apartments
- Ridgepool View (Wheelchair Accessible)
- Kinhart's Moy Estuary House
- The Old Deanery Holiday Cottages
- Killala Holiday Village
- Sea Stack View

Campsites

Belleek Park Caravan & Camping
Open from March to October, with prior arrangement for the rest of the year, the park provides free WiFi, season pitches for tourers, sites for new mobile homes, and secure storage options.
-> F26 YY58. Dog-friendly. ///misled.detector.runway

Atlantic Caravan Park
The Atlantic Caravan Park, located on the breathtaking beachfront of Killala Bay in Enniscrone, is an exceptional family-run caravan park. With stunning views, natural sand dunes, and 5km of pristine beaches, it offers a truly remarkable experience.
-> F26 PY54. Dog-friendly. ///insight.bunches.respect

Gortnor Abbey Pier Aire
Situated by the waterfront, visitors can enjoy beautiful views and a peaceful atmosphere. With convenient services and amenities available, Gortnor Abbey Pier provides a comfortable and enjoyable stopover for up to 8 vehicles to spend the night.
-> F26 FA09. Wheelchair accessible. Dog-friendly. ///consulted.wasps.toothpick

Roadtrip Essentials
in Erris

Food Shops
- Aldi, Ballina
- Lidl, Ballina
- Costcutter, Ballina
- Londis, Hineys
- Spar, Barnatra
- Centra, Bangor Erris

Water Points and CDP
- Certa Services Culleens (Water Only)
- Ballina Port (Water Only)
- Belmullet Tidal Pool (Water only)
- Marty's Halfay House (Water & CDP)

Electric Vehicle Charging Points
- Monta Charging Station, Quay Road, Quignalecka ///tallest.tripled.judged
- Community by Shell Recharge Charging Station: Talagh Rd, Belmullet ///talked.module.vetera
- Tesla Destination Charger: Broadhaven Bay Hotel ///enthusiasts.postnatal.expanded
- ecars Charge Point, Main Street, Belmullet ///fortitude.annul.retraining

SIGHTS

Viewpoints
- 47. Annagh Head
- 52. White Cliffs of Ashleam
- 57. Moyteoge Head

Beaches & Harbours
- 48. Elly bay Beach
- 53. Ashleam Bay
- 56. Keem Strand
- 59. Dugort Beach
- 61. Mulranny beach

Island
- 49. Claggan Island
- 51. Inishbiggle

Nature Spots
- 50. Wild Nephin National Park

Walks
- 54. Woodland Faerie Trail

Castles & Historical Sights
- 55. Achill-Henge
- 58. Rockfleet Castle
- 60. Kildavnet Tower

Achill Island and Clew Bay

The charming landscapes of Achill Island and Clew Bay invite you to discover the beauty of Ireland's wild western coastline. There are stories of ancient legends that lie here, and the impressive cliffs and untouched beaches create a sense of wonder. In this captivating setting, the bright colours of the heathlands and rolling hills showcase Ireland's stunning natural beauty.

Stroll through the friendly communities, where Irish warmth welcomes you, and the rich history of Achill Island and Clew Bay surrounds you. The region's beautiful scenery has inspired many artists and dreamers, leaving a strong impression on everyone who explores its lovely pathways. As you walk along the stormy shores, the powerful waves of the Atlantic Ocean remind you of nature's strength and timeless appeal.

Achill Island and Clew Bay is a beautiful part of this wild Atlantic coastal route that will leave you with memories for years to come.

In order to reach these outer isles, the closest airport is in the northern town of Sligo. You can also reach this area easily by public transport, transiting to Ballina by train and then changing to the local bus service. You can also rent a car from here and drive out to the coastline.

Achill Island and Clew Bay, set along the captivating western coast of Ireland, unveil a mesmerising blend of dramatic landscapes, captivating history, and a rich cultural tapestry. This picturesque area is defined by its awe-inspiring coastline, untouched beaches, and majestic mountains, providing a perfect backdrop for the quaint towns and villages scattered throughout the region.

The area's vibrant cultural mosaic is steeped in ancient legends and traditions, igniting the imagination of artists and poets. At the heart of Achill Island and Clew Bay, the inviting villages radiate warmth and hospitality, enticing travelers to delve into the local arts and crafts scene, which showcases the finest examples of traditional Irish craftsmanship. With its irresistible combination of natural beauty, history, and culture, Achill Island and Clew Bay form an enchanting destination that encourages travellers to explore and create cherished memories.

56 KEEM STRAND

47. Annagh Head

Perched on the rugged coastline of County Mayo, a breathtaking viewpoint offers panoramic vistas of the wild Atlantic Ocean. Annagh Head, with its dramatic cliffs and crashing waves, is a testament to nature's raw power and beauty.

The salty sea breeze and the sound of seabirds soaring overhead create an unforgettable sensory experience for visitors seeking to connect with Ireland's untamed landscape.

-> Follow the R313 from Belmullet towards Blacksod and turn left onto L1203. Continue along this road until you arrive. ///patriot.oats.microwaves

48. Elly Bay Beach

Nestled along the picturesque coastline, a tranquil oasis of pristine sands and crystalline waters welcomes visitors to the idyllic Elly Bay beach. This serene haven provides an escape from the hustle and bustle of daily life, where the gentle lapping of waves and the soothing embrace of the sea breeze create an atmosphere of calm and rejuvenation.

The beach's unspoiled beauty beckons nature lovers and those seeking respite alike, while the surrounding area offers opportunities for leisurely strolls, birdwatching, and simply basking in the breathtaking scenery.

-> Follow the R313 road from Belmullet, and then turn onto the L1202 road. Continue until you arrive. Wheelchair accessible. Dog-friendly. ///conjured.overtakes.retro

48 ELLY BAY BEACH

49. Claggan Island

Surrounded by the rugged beauty of the Atlantic Ocean, the enchanting Claggan Island offers a unique and unforgettable experience for visitors seeking both adventure and tranquility. Its striking landscape, peppered with charming cottages and windswept terrain, creates a sense of timelessness and connection to Ireland's rich cultural heritage. The island's unspoiled beauty, coupled with its warm and welcoming community, ensures a truly captivating experience for all who visit.

-> Drive along the R313 road from Belmullet and turn right onto the L1205 road. Continue until you arrive at the causeway connecting the island to the mainland. Dog-friendly. ///chessboard.lowered.nurseries

50. Wild Nephin National Park

Immersed in the untamed wilderness of Western Ireland lies a haven for nature enthusiasts and adventure-seekers: Wild Nephin National Park. This vast expanse of forests, mountains, and bogs offers a breathtaking backdrop for outdoor activities such as hiking and wildlife spotting. The park's unspoiled beauty and diverse landscapes provide a unique opportunity for visitors to reconnect with nature and explore the captivating terrain.

-> Take the N59 road from Newport and follow the signs directing you to the park. Wheelchair-accessible. Dog-friendly. ///thus.antidotes.imbued

51. Inishbiggle

Tucked between the shores of Achill Island and the mainland, the enchanting island of Inishbiggle offers visitors an authentic glimpse into traditional Irish life. Its unspoiled beauty, combined with a rich history and a warm, welcoming community, creates a truly captivating experience for those who venture to this secluded haven. The island's tranquil atmosphere and stunning landscapes provide the perfect setting for relaxation, reflection, and exploration.

-> Take a ferry from either Achill Island or the mainland at Doran's Point. ///emulate.geography.butlers

50 WILD NEPHIN NATIONAL PARK

52 WHITE CLIFFS OF ASHLEAM

52. White Cliffs of Ashleam

Rising majestically along the rugged coastline, the incredible White Cliffs of Ashleam stand as a testament to the raw beauty of the Wild Atlantic Way. These dramatic limestone cliffs captivate visitors with their breathtaking views of the ocean and surrounding landscapes.

A visit to this natural wonder provides an unforgettable experience, where the powerful forces of nature are on full display. A handy tip for visiting: wear comfortable shoes with good grip, as the terrain can be uneven and slippery, especially in wet conditions.

-> Drive along the N59 road from Mulranny towards Achill Island, and then follow the signs for Ashleam. Wheelchair-Accessible. Dog-friendly. ///causing.monitored.moved

53. Ashleam Bay

A hidden gem nestled along the rugged coastline, the picturesque Ashleam Bay offers a serene escape for those seeking peace and natural beauty. The bay's pristine sands and clear waters create a tranquil haven, perfect for unwinding and reconnecting with the splendour of nature. Its breathtaking views and peaceful atmosphere make Ashleam Bay an idyllic destination for relaxation, leisurely strolls, and quiet contemplation.

-> Drive along the N59 road from Mulranny towards Achill Island and follow the signs for Ashleam. Dog-friendly. ///before.turtles.liaise

54. Woodland Faerie Trail

Immerse yourself in the enchanting world of the Woodland Faerie Trail on Achill Island, where magic and nature intertwine to create a delightful experience for all ages. This playful trail weaves through lush woodlands, with charming faerie houses, delightful sculptures, and captivating surprises awaiting around every bend. A true haven for the imagination, the Woodland Faerie Trail invites visitors to explore, dream, and reconnect with the wonder of nature.

->Drive along the N59 road from Mulranny towards Achill Island and follow the signs for the trail. ///lullabies.thorny.rank

56 KEEM STRAND

55. Achill-Henge
Steeped in intrigue and controversy, the enigmatic structure known as Achill-Henge stands as a testament to the enduring power of artistic expression. This modern-day Stonehenge, constructed in 2011 by Joe McNamara, has captured the imagination of visitors with its mysterious presence and striking design.

The monument's history is shrouded in legal battles, as it was built without planning permission, adding an air of defiance and rebellion to its allure.

-> Park nearby the St Patrick's Church between Dooagh and Keel and take the road up the hill to the west of the church. Follow the sign posts all the way to the monument. Do not drive to it as the road is narrow. ///shrimp.sugars.fulfilling

56. Keem Strand
Nestled between towering cliffs and the azure waters of the Atlantic Ocean, the breathtaking Keem Strand offers visitors a tranquil escape amidst the raw beauty of nature.

This sheltered, horseshoe-shaped beach will come into view as you drive along the cliffside road. The pristine sands and crystal-clear waters, provide an idyllic setting for relaxing on the sand, swimming, and leisurely strolls. The surrounding landscapes and breathtaking views make Keem Strand a must-visit destination for visitors.

-> Drive along the N59 road towards Achill Island, and follow the signs for Keem Bay. Wheelchair accessible. Dog-friendly. ///extends.hockey.banker

57. Moyteoge Head

Perched high above the rugged coastline, Moyteoge Head offers visitors a breathtaking panorama of the Wild Atlantic Way's untamed beauty. With its dramatic cliffs and sweeping views of the ocean, this stunning vantage point is the perfect destination for photographers, nature enthusiasts, and those seeking solace in the embrace of the elements. The captivating scenery and invigorating sea breeze create an unforgettable experience for all who venture to this mesmerising location.

-> *Drive along the N59 road towards Achill Island, and follow the signs directing you to the viewpoint. ///placidly.shatters.pacers*

58. Rockfleet Castle

Standing sentinel over the shores of Clew Bay, the imposing Rockfleet Castle whispers tales of a bygone era, when pirates and chieftains ruled the waves. This 16th-century tower house, also known as Carrickahowley Castle, was once the stronghold of the legendary pirate queen, Grace O'Malley.

Steeped in history and intrigue, the castle's storied past and atmospheric presence continue to captivate the imaginations of visitors from near and far.

-> *Drive along the N59 road from Westport towards Newport, and follow the signs for the castle. Dog-friendly. ///immaculately.unexpectedly.gift*

59. Dugort Beach

A tranquil oasis along the rugged coastline of Achill Island, the pristine sands of Dugort Beach beckon visitors seeking solace and rejuvenation. This Blue Flag beach, with its crystal-clear waters and breathtaking mountain backdrop, provides the perfect setting for relaxation, swimming, and leisurely strolls.

The beach's serene atmosphere is further enhanced by the nearby Dugort village, with its charming thatched cottages and warm hospitality. Bring a picnic to enjoy on the beach, as the stunning views make for an unforgettable al fresco dining experience.

-> *Drive along the N59 road from Mulranny towards Achill Island, and follow the signs for Dugort. Wheelchair accessible. Dog-friendly. ///slewed.added.intro*

59 DUGORT BEACH

55 ACHILL-HENGE

60. Kildavnet Tower

Standing proudly along the rugged coastline, the enigmatic Kildavnet Tower bears witness to centuries of history and intrigue. This 15th-century tower, also known as Grace O'Malley's Castle, once served as a strategic stronghold for the legendary pirate queen.

Today, the tower's imposing silhouette and storied past continue to captivate the imaginations of visitors from near and far. As you explore this historic landmark, you can almost hear the echoes of ancient battles and daring seafaring adventures.

-> *Drive along the N59 road from Mulranny towards Achill Island, and follow the signs directing you to the site. Dog-friendly. ///posies.frustrations.conductor*

61. Mulranny beach

A hidden gem along the Wild Atlantic Way, the enchanting Mulranny Beach offers a serene retreat amidst breathtaking natural beauty. With its pristine sands, crystal-clear waters, and stunning views of Clew Bay and Croagh Patrick, this picturesque beach provides the perfect setting for relaxation, swimming, and leisurely strolls. The surrounding landscapes and vibrant flora create an unforgettable experience for all who venture to this tranquil haven.

-> *Drive along the N59 road from Westport towards Mulranny, and follow the signs for the beach. Wheelchair accessible. Dog-friendly. Height barrier 2m at entrance. ///twigs.baffles.manicures*

61 MULRANNY BEACH

Where to Eat
on Achill Island and Clew Bay

Mc's Bistro & Grill
With experienced chefs serving mouth-watering dishes from their à la carte menu as well as daily specials and homemade desserts, it is a must-visit destination for food lovers. Boasting a modern atmosphere and open for breakfast, lunch, and dinner, Mc's Bistro & Grill provides exceptional service.

-> *F25 W5HO. ///belt.touted.girder*

Nephin Restaurant
Nephin Restaurant, located at the 4-star Mulranny Park Hotel in Westport, Co Mayo, offers exquisite world-class cuisine. As an award-winning establishment, it is a must-visit destination for those seeking a remarkable dining experience.

-> *F28 N2H9. ///reckon.preset.skirts*

The Cross, Achill Island
The Cross, located on Achill Island in County Mayo, is a highly-rated restaurant. With a diverse menu and excellent customer reviews, it is a top choice for those seeking a memorable dining experience in a beautiful coastal setting.

-> *Wheelchair Accessible. F28 D7P8 ///creations.framework.workloads*

The Currach
Sitting on the remote and breathtaking Achill Island, the Currach sits overlooking the beautiful stretch of sand known as Keel Beach. With deliciously prepared dishes, friendly staff, and stunningly bright interiors, this hidden gem in Achill offers an unforgettable dining experience.

-> *F28 TX96. ///carpeted.tempted.acrobats*

Nevin's Newfield Inn
Nevins Inn captures the essence of Irish hospitality with its historic charm and breathtaking views of Clew Bay and Nephin mountain. From homely lounge serving reasonably priced, high-standard, homemade bar food it offers a truly revitalising experience in an award-winning establishment.

-> *F28 56K1. Wheelchair accessible. ///electrodes.promote.eyebrows*

Stone Barn Cafe
As a lover of exquisite vegetarian cuisine, the Stone Barn Cafe on Clare Island captures hearts from around the world. With a seasonal menu of delicious soups, creative mains, and fresh garden salads, alongside indulgent cakes, this cosy establishment prioritises high-quality, organic ingredients.

->*F28 CF68. ///resent.eclipses.implicitly*

Where to Stay
on Achill Island and Clew Bay

Hotels
- Geraghtys Farmyard Pods
- Further Space at Belmullet (Wheelchair Accessible)
- The Western Strands Guesthouse
- Murrayville B&B (Dog-friendly)
- Lavelles Seaside House
- Teach Cruachan B&B (Wheelchair Accessible. Dog-friendly)

Self-Catering Apartments
- Doolough Dream (Wheelchair Accessible)
- Leam Cottage
- M033 Achill Gatehouse (Wheelchair Accessible)
- Clew Bay Cottage
- Avondale House (Wheelchair Accessible)
- Lavelle's Seaside House
- Greystone House

Campsites

Achill Seal Caves Campsite
Get ready to embark on a memorable camping experience at Seal Caves. With a variety of pitches that cater to different needs, including options for families or groups, this well-sheltered park surrounded by nature offers the perfect setting. Dog lovers will appreciate the ideal environment.
-> F28 P273. Dog-friendly. ///baking.advertises.limousines

Keel Camping
Keel Camping offers a range of pitch options for motorhomes, campervans, caravans, and tents, all overlooking the breathtaking Keel Beach. The friendly staff ensures a seamless experience, guiding new guests to their designated area. Electrical hookups are available for those who've booked them.
> F28 CA47. Wheelchair accessible. Dog-friendly. ///outlet.contacted.louts

Nevins Motorhome Park
The Nevins Motorhome car park, located opposite the Newfield Inn premises, offering well-equipped spaces with electricity, water, and CCTV. This is the perfect Aire for those seeking affordable parking nearby a cosy pub.
-> F28 56K1. Dog-friendly. ///electrodes.promote.eyebrows

Roadtrip Essentials
on Achill Island and Clew Bay

Food Shops
- EuroSpar, Belmullet
- McGloin's Gala
- Centra, Bangor
- Sweeney's SuperValu Achill
- Doherty's Costcutter

Water Points and CDP
- Blacksod Lighthouse (Water Only)
- Mulranny Railway Station (Water Only)
- Hy Breasal B&B (Water & CDP)
- Circle K, Cashel (Water Only)
- Keel Beach Car Park (Water Only)

Electric Vehicle Charging Points
- Community by Shell Recharge Charging Station, Talagh Rd, Belmullet: ///talked.module.veteran
- ecars Charge Point, Main Street, Belmullet ///fortitude.annul.retraining
- Tesla Destination Charger, Broadhaven Bay Hotel ///enthusiasts.postnatal.expanded
- EVBox Charging Station, Ballycroy Visitor Centre ///cheeks.vaccine.recorded
- ecars Charge Point, Westport Plaza Hotel ///unifies.toners.bobble
- ePower Charging Station, Knockranny ///linger.speaking.cuddles
- ESB Charging Station, Circle K Service Station ///scatter.gasping.lemmings
- ecars Charge Point, James Street, Westport ///amazed.keeps.airline

56 KEEM STRAND

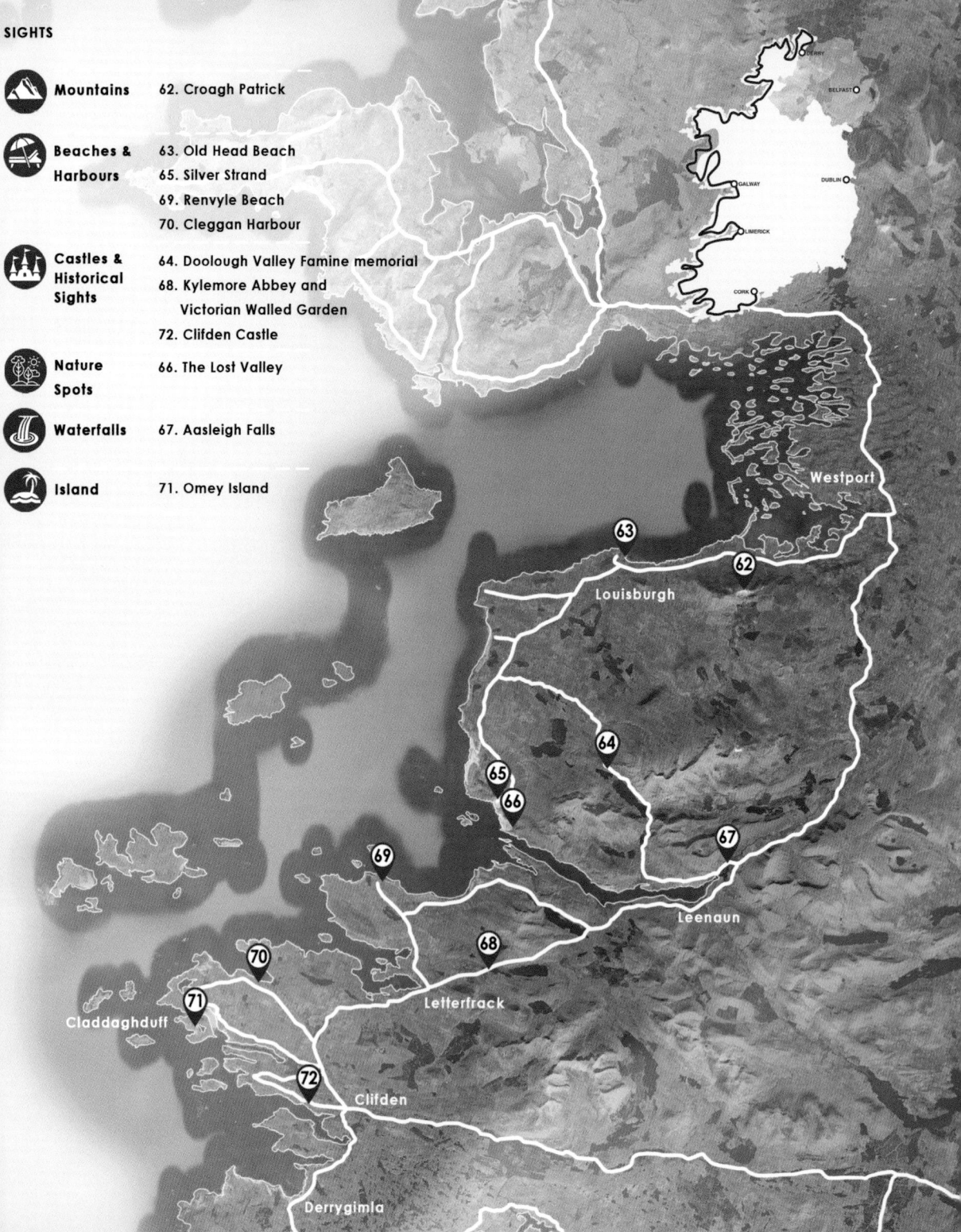

Killary Harbour

Nestled in the mesmerising heart of the Wild Atlantic Way lies the Killary Harbour region, a fascinating destination where nature's grandeur is on full display. Rich in folklore and cultural heritage, Killary Harbour invites visitors to immerse themselves in Ireland's fascinating history through its ancient remains, grand castles, and time-honoured churches.

Beyond its historical charm, Killary Harbour is home to some of Ireland's most breathtaking landscapes. From the dramatic slopes of Mweelrea Mountain to the tranquil waters of Ireland's only fjord, the region's beauty is truly unrivalled.

The diverse terrain of Killary Harbour is a paradise for outdoor enthusiasts, who are drawn to its striking coastline, soaring cliffs, and hidden coves. Adventure seekers can hike, cycle, or kayak along the coast, discovering beautiful views and undiscovered treasures at every turn.

Of course, the beaches are equally magnificent. From the unspoiled sands of Old Head Beach to the secluded charm of Silver Strand, Killary Harbour boasts some of the most stunning beaches in Ireland. It's not only the idyllic shores that enchant you – it's the profound sense of serenity that emerges from being surrounded by such extraordinary natural beauty.

In order to reach this region, the closest airports are in Sligo to the north or Connemara to the south. You can reach this area easily by public transport, transiting to Westport by train and then changing to the local bus service. You can also rent a car from here and drive out to the coastline.

Visitors to Killary Harbour can expect a truly immersive experience that combines breathtaking natural beauty with a wealth of outdoor activities and a rich cultural heritage. As Ireland's only fjord, Killary Harbour stretches for 16 kilometres, offering unparalleled views of the rugged Connemara landscape.

The surrounding mountains, such as Mweelrea and the Twelve Bens, create a dramatic backdrop that captivates the senses and will leave you saying "wow" at every turn. The region's diverse terrain, from its memorable coastline and towering cliffs to hidden coves and immaculate beaches, provides ample opportunities for exploration and adventure.

A trip to Killary Harbour is not complete without indulging in the vast array of outdoor activities available to visitors. Hiking, cycling, and kayaking are popular pursuits, allowing you to fully appreciate the stunning scenery and uncover hidden gems along the way. For those interested in marine life, boat tours offer the chance to spot dolphins, seals, and a variety of seabirds.

64 DOOLOUGH VALLEY FAMINE MEMORIAL

62. Croagh Patrick

Rising majestically above the surrounding landscape, this sacred mountain holds a special place in the hearts of both locals and visitors alike. Revered as Ireland's holiest peak, Croagh Patrick has been a pilgrimage site for centuries, drawing spiritual seekers and avid hikers to its slopes.

A 7km out and back walk will take you 764m high above the stunning Clew Bay and the rolling hills of County Mayo. The stunning views make the challenging ascent well worth the effort. A visit to this iconic mountain offers a unique blend of spiritual connection, physical challenge, and awe-inspiring vistas that create lasting memories.

-> Travel to the village of Murrisk, situated 8 kms west of Westport on the R335 road. The well-marked trailhead and car park are located just off the main road. ///enacted.unworn.repeal

63. Old Head Beach

Nestled along the picturesque shores of County Mayo, this idyllic stretch of sand and sea offers a tranquil retreat for beach lovers and families alike. Old Head Beach, with its golden sands and azure waters, provides the perfect setting for a relaxing day of sunbathing, swimming, or building sandcastles.

The breathtaking views of Croagh Patrick and the surrounding countryside add to the beach's enchanting atmosphere, making it an ideal spot to unwind and soak in the beauty of the Wild Atlantic Way.

-> Follow the R335 road from Westport towards Louisburgh for 13kms. Continue west on the R378 for 3 kms, you will find the beach on your left. Wheelchair accessible. Dog-friendly. ///mighty.weeping.refine

63 OLD HEAD BEACH

64 DOOLOUGH VALLEY FAMINE MEMORIAL

64. Doolough Valley Famine Memorial

Steeped in a poignant history, this evocative memorial stands as a testament to the resilience and strength of the Irish people during the Great Famine. Located in the hauntingly beautiful Doolough Valley, the Famine memorial commemorates the tragic Doolough Tragedy of 1849, when hundreds of starving people perished during a desperate walk in search of food and assistance.

The stark, rugged landscape surrounding the memorial serves as a powerful reminder of the hardships endured by those who suffered through one of Ireland's darkest periods.

-> Take the N59 road towards Leenane. At the village of Drummin, turn left onto the R335 road and continue for 9kms to reach the memorial site. Wheelchair accessible. Dog-friendly. ///pumas.readings.calls

65. Silver Strand
Tucked away in the breathtaking Killary Harbour, this hidden gem of a beach offers a serene escape for those seeking solace in nature. Silver Strand, with its pristine white sands and crystal-clear waters, is surrounded by dramatic cliffs and lush greenery, creating an awe-inspiring atmosphere. The secluded location makes it a perfect spot for a peaceful picnic, leisurely swim, or quiet contemplation while admiring the stunning surroundings.

-> Follow the N59 road towards Leenane, and then take the R336 road towards Tully Cross. Continue and turn left onto a local road at the signpost for Silver Strand. The final stretch of the journey involves a narrow, winding road. Dog-friendly. ///tenses.testify.silent

66. The Lost Valley
Nestled amidst the majestic mountains of Killary Harbour, a secluded treasure steeped in history and natural beauty awaits exploration. Known as The Lost Valley, this untouched haven offers visitors a rare glimpse into the authentic Irish countryside, while also providing the opportunity to delve into its rich heritage.

The pristine landscape, characterised by its lush green pastures, cascading waterfalls, and ancient stone walls, serves as a living testament to the resilience and perseverance of the families who once called this valley home during the Great Famine.

This is only accessible by a private tour and must be booked in advance. Check the availability online for the full details of the tour.

-> Take the N59 road from Westport towards Leenane, and then turn onto the R335 road towards Louisburgh. Follow the signs for The Lost Valley from Louisburgh. Entrance sits beside Silver Strand car park. ///acids.underclass.lockup

67. Aasleigh Falls
In the heart of County Mayo, a thundering cascade captivates visitors with its raw power and mesmerizing beauty. Aasleigh Falls, located along the Erriff River, provides a stunning spectacle as the water tumbles over the rugged rocks, creating an invigorating atmosphere.

The falls are a renowned destination for anglers, as the Erriff River is home to a thriving population of wild Atlantic salmon, making it an angler's paradise.

-> Take the N59 road towards Leenane. 7kms before Leenane, turn left onto a local road following the signs for Aasleigh Falls. Dog-friendly. ///kidding.vegetarian.secondary

68 KYLEMORE ABBEY AND VICTORIAN WALLED

68. Kylemore Abbey and Victorian Walled Garden

Amidst the breathtaking beauty of Connemara lies a breathtaking mansion that dates back to the 19th century, founded for Benedictine Nuns who fled Belgium in World War I. The nuns opened up a school for local girls and an international boarding school during this time.

Kylemore Abbey has an interactive visitor experience where you can learn about the stories and tales of the generations that lived here over the years.

-> *Take the N59 road from Westport towards Clifden. The entrance to the estate is situated 15kms west of Leenane. Wheelchair accessible.*
///face.bobble.antiseptic

69. Renvyle Beach

Embraced by the rugged beauty of Connemara's coastline, a pristine stretch of sand and crystal-clear waters beckons visitors seeking tranquility and natural splendour. Renvyle Beach, with its panoramic views of the Atlantic Ocean and the surrounding mountains, is a haven for those yearning to connect with the wild, untamed beauty of the Irish landscape.

Interestingly, the nearby Renvyle Peninsula is home to an abundance of historical sites, including a 13th-century castle that once belonged to the pirate queen Grace O'Malley.

-> *Take the N59 road from Westport towards Clifden and then turn onto the R344 road towards Tully Cross. Follow the signs for Renvyle Beach from Tully Cross. Wheelchair accessible. Dog-friendly. ///rocketing.shank.crumples*

70. Cleggan Harbour

Bustling with activity and brimming with charm, this picturesque coastal village in Connemara boasts a lively harbour that serves as a gateway to the inviting islands of Inishbofin and Inishturk.

Cleggan Harbour, with its idyllic surroundings and a rich maritime history, is a hub for fishing boats, ferries, and pleasure crafts. The nearby Cleggan Head is home to the remains of a prehistoric fort, revealing the area's ancient past.

-> Take the N59 road towards Clifden, and then turn onto the R341 road towards Cleggan. The harbour is located in the heart of the village. Wheelchair accessible. Dog-friendly. ///tonight.rainstorm.rituals

71. Omey Island

A hidden gem tucked away along the rugged Connemara coastline, a tidal island reveals its fascinating history and breathtaking landscapes at low tide. Omey Island, steeped in ancient legends and adorned with pristine beaches, offers visitors an unforgettable experience as they explore the remnants of a monastic settlement and a submerged village. The island was once home to the last pagan king of Ireland, who converted to Christianity in the 7th century.

-> Take the N59 road towards Clifden, and then turn onto the R341 road towards Cleggan. Follow the signs for Claddaghduff and Omey Island. Dog-friendly. ///normality.negotiable.atomic

68 KYLEMORE ABBEY AND VICTORIAN WALLED

72. Clifden Castle

Enveloped by the untamed allure of Connemara, the eerie remains of a once-magnificent Gothic Revival castle stir the imagination with an air of secrecy and enchantment. Clifden Castle, formerly an emblem of splendour and extravagance, now bears witness to the relentless march of time.

Constructed in the early 1800s, the castle served as the inaugural dwelling in the town of Clifden, a settlement established by the castle's initial proprietor, John D'Arcy.

-> *Upon entering Clifden, follow the signs for the Sky Road and Clifden Castle. Dog-friendly. ///coastal.unfiltered.flinch*

Where to Eat
in Killary Harbour

Cronin's Sheebeen
A traditional award-winning pub and restaurant located just outside Westport, overlooking Clew Bay and near Westport Harbour. With a strong reputation for quality food, it is recognised as one of the top bar restaurants on the west coast of Ireland.

-> F28 VK70. Dog-friendly. ///scrub.unclip.steep

The Towers Bar & Restaurant
Guests can join experienced skipper Tom aboard the fishing vessel "White Water II" to explore Clew Bay and catch their own dinner. Upon returning, the talented chefs at The Towers will be happy to cook guests' catch, adding a personalised touch to the dining experience.

-> F29 V650. Wheelchair Accessible. ///baggage.treehouse.cursed

Louisburgh 74 - Café Bistro
With delicious food, friendly service, and a quirky atmosphere, the cafe offers a great menu selection, including fish chowder, salmon bagels, and tasty baked goods. Visitors especially appreciate the welcoming staff, cosy ambiance, and the option to browse second-hand books. Overall, it is described as a hidden gem and a delightful spot in Louisburgh.

-> F28 W5X6. Wheelchair Accessible. ///craving.duplicated.devout

Mitchell's Restaurant
Highly regarded for its speciality in seafood dishes, along with top-quality meat and vegetarian options. Located in the charming seaside town, Mitchell's offers a delightful culinary experience with a focus on fresh and flavourful cuisine.

-> H71 WT32. ///race.breed.budding

Lowry's Bar
An authentic Irish pub that combines live music with a wide selection of whiskey and gin. Renowned for its wholesome and delicious pub food, Lowry's Bar has been serving its famous toasted sandwiches for over half a century.

-> H71 WT32. Wheelchair Accessible. ///enjoy.banter.filer

Little Fish Cafe, Cleggan
Little Fish Cafe in Cleggan, County Galway is a must-visit spot known for its fresh seafood dishes. With a focus on locally-sourced ingredients, it has quickly become one of the greatest small restaurants of the year. Check out their daily menu updates on their Instagram page.

-> H71 E680. ///speech.forming.unseen

Where to Stay
in Killary Harbour

Hotels
- Ardmore Country House Hotel
- Westport Coast Hotel (Wheelchair Accessible)
- Delphi Resort (Wheelchair Accessible)
- Wild Atlantic Hostel (Wheelchair Accessible)
- All the Twos Guesthouse
- Hazelbrook Farmhouse B&B

Self-Catering Apartments
- Asgard Apartments
- Delphi Lodge (Dog-friendly)
- Murrisk Apartments
- Devlin Farm Life (Wheelchair Accessible)
- Renvyle 353 Kylemore Lake Cottage (Dog-friendly)
- Red Deer Cottage
- Once Upon a Tide (Wheelchair Accessible. Dog-friendly)

Campsites

Connemara Camping
Connemara Camping Park provides a peaceful and secluded location in the middle of Connemara, with its own beach and picturesque alcoves. Clean facilities, a on-site shop, and a quiet atmosphere make it a delightful camping experience.
-> H91 NR13. Dog-friendly. ///paperbacks.befits.handed

Clifden Eco Beach
As an eco-certified carbon-neutral establishment, it offers breathtaking sea views, secluded sandy beaches, spacious pitches, and a serene atmosphere, allowing visitors to immerse themselves in nature while enjoying activities on the water.
-> H71 W024. Dog-friendly. ///mastering.attune.trapdoor

Renvyle Beach Campsite
With 36 pitches catering to tents and caravans, the park is a perfect escape for families. Direct access to a beautiful sandy beach, stunning views of picturesque islands, and environmental excellence make it an ideal spot to relax and unwind.
-> H91 R2YC. ///preserves.halves.delirious

63 OLD HEAD BEACH

Roadtrip Essentials
in Killary Harbour

Food Shops
- Centra, Westport
- Rogan's Mace Renvyle
- Letterfrack Country Shop
- Rogan's, Cleggan
- Aldi, Clifden
- Lidl, Clifden

Water Points and CDP
- Marty's Halfway House (Water & CDP)
- Old Head Beach (Water Only)
- Louisburgh Services (Water Only)
- Carrownisky Beach (Water Only)
- Leenaun High Street (Water Only)
- Derryherbert Pier (Water Only)
- Clifden Public Toilets (Water Only)
- Aughrus Pier (Water Only)

Electric Vehicle Charging Points
- ecars Charge Point, James Street, Westport: ///amazed.keeps.airline
- ecars Charge Point, Westport Plaza Hotel ///unifies.toners.bobble
- EasyGo Charging Station, Westport Quay ///weaving.metering.exposed
- ESB Charging Station, Station House Courtyard, Galway Rd ///fancy.sorry.include
- EVBox Charging Station, Connemara NP visitor Centre ///undermines.fulfilling.undulation
- Tesla Destination Charger, Renvyle House Hotel ///gaining.lamb.unseal
- ecars Charge Point: Dolphin Beach House, Belleek ///wading.crest.folktales
- ecars Charge Point, Abbeyglen Castle Hotel ///reduce.lowest.perform

72 CLIFDEN CASTLE

Connemara

In the heart of the West of Ireland, the wild and untamed landscape of Connemara tells the ancient stories of its people, cradled between the mountains and the sea. A land of contrasts, Connemara's ethereal beauty is painted with a palette of vibrant greens, deep blues, and shimmering silver, as the ever-changing light dances across the rolling hills and rugged coastline.

Here, the echoes of history reverberate through the stone walls and thatched cottages, where the mountains themselves have stories to tell, and the music of fiddles and guitars fills the air in the cosy warmth of village pubs. The soul of Connemara is a wild and passionate spirit, a testament to the resilience and strength of the people who have carved their lives from this enchanting land.

As the wind whispers through the heather and the waves crash against the shore, one cannot help but feel the powerful connection between land and sea, past and present, and the eternal beauty of Ireland's western jewel.

In order to reach this region, the closest airports is at Connemara airport to the south. You can reach this area easily by public transport, transiting to Galway by train and then changing to the local bus service. You can also rent a car from here and drive out to the coastline.

Connemara is a region in County Galway, characterised by its unique landscape, rich cultural heritage, and numerous attractions for visitors. Some of the most popular sites include the Connemara National Park, a vast expanse of protected land featuring diverse flora and fauna, as well as hiking trails and stunning vistas of the Twelve Bens mountain range.

The picturesque village of Clifden, often considered the capital of Connemara, offers a variety of accommodations, dining options, and shopping opportunities, as well as easy access to the nearby Sky Road, a scenic driving route with panoramic views of the coastline. For history enthusiasts, the impressive Kylemore Abbey and Victorian Walled Garden provide a fascinating glimpse into the past, while the nearby village of Leenane hosts the Sheep and Wool Centre, showcasing traditional sheep farming and wool production techniques.

74 DOG'S BAY

73. Connemara National park

Nestled within the rugged beauty of Ireland's western coast lies an enchanting haven of natural beauty and rich heritage. This captivating expanse, known as Connemara National Park, spans over 2,000 hectares of unspoiled landscapes, from boglands to mountains.

Home to the iconic Twelve Bens mountain range, the park provides a sanctuary for unique flora and fauna, including the protected Connemara pony. The fusion of awe-inspiring scenery and fascinating history creates an unforgettable experience for all who visit.

-> *Follow the N59 from Galway City or Clifden. Wheelchair accessible. Dog-friendly.*
///visual.interacted.homemakers

74. Dog's Bay

A crescent-shaped haven of pristine beauty, Dog's Bay boasts a stretch of powdery white sands and crystal-clear waters along Ireland's western coast. This idyllic beach, renowned for its unique composition of crushed seashells, offers a serene escape from the bustle of daily life. Surrounded by vibrant flora and fauna, the unspoiled shoreline provides a picturesque setting for leisurely strolls, picnics, and water-based activities.

-> *From Roundstone, follow the signs for Dog's Bay, located approximately 3km away. Dog-friendly.*
///helps.sidelines.wasting

75. Roundstone

Tucked away on the rugged shores of Ireland's western coast, the picturesque village of Roundstone offers a delightful blend of charm, history, and natural beauty. As a hub of traditional Irish craftsmanship, Roundstone is famed for its skilled bodhrán makers, whose handcrafted drums have been cherished by musicians worldwide.

With its colourful houses and bustling harbour, the village exudes an inviting atmosphere that captivates the hearts of visitors.

-> *Take the R341 from Clifden, following the signs to the village. Wheelchair accessible. Dog-friendly. ///oldie.sprang.cheekbones*

76. Spiddal Pier

Nestled along the picturesque shores of Galway Bay, the quaint Spiddal Pier serves as a gateway to the wild beauty of the Atlantic Ocean. This charming location is renowned for its vibrant marine life, making it an ideal spot for fishing enthusiasts and nature lovers alike.

The pier's breathtaking views of the Aran Islands and the distant Cliffs of Moher provide a mesmerising backdrop for leisurely strolls and photography.

-> *Follow the R336 from Galway City towards Spiddal village then follow signs to the pier. Wheelchair accessible. Dog-friendly. ///eyelashes.recalls.felling*

76 SPIDDAL PIER

77. Mutton Island
Steeped in history and natural beauty, Mutton Island stands proudly off the coast of Galway City, offering a unique glimpse into Ireland's maritime past. Home to an ancient monastic settlement and a 19th-century lighthouse, this small isle has long been a beacon for seafarers navigating the Atlantic waters. A haven for birdwatchers, the island hosts a variety of seabird species, making it a true wildlife sanctuary.

-> Tickets to visit Mutton Island can be booked through local tour operators by a guided boat. ///drips.sheets.kicks

78. Silverstrand Beach
A secluded oasis on the outskirts of Galway City, Silverstrand Beach beckons visitors with its golden sands and gentle waves. This sheltered cove, framed by rocky cliffs, provides a serene setting for relaxation and water-based activities. The beach's unique tidal patterns create a mesmerising interplay of light and water, offering a visual spectacle that enchants photographers and nature enthusiasts alike.

-> Follow the R336 from Galway City towards Barna, then turn onto the R292, following signs to the beach. Wheelchair accessible. Dog-friendly. ///compel.tweed.tiger

Where to Eat
in Connemara

Owenmore Restaurant
Ballynahinch Castle's Owenmore Restaurant in Connemara, Ireland, offers fine dining with stunning views of the river and woodland. The elegant dining room features an impressive art collection. The restaurant caters to dietary requirements and specialises in pure Irish delicacies.

-> H91 F4A7. Wheelchair Accessible
///birdhouse.essentially.markets

Signal Bar and Restaurant
This restaurant exudes an old-world charm within the original Clifden Railway Station. With a relaxed atmosphere, it offers a menu featuring carefully sourced ingredients, from seafood chowder to Connemara lamb shank. Enjoy a delightful dining experience in this unique setting.

-> H71 PX68. ///tonic.torn.recently

Tigh Mheaic
A traditional Irish bar and restaurant with a modern twist, is located in scenic Carna, Co. Galway. They offer locally sourced food, catering to various dietary requirements, and provide a warm, friendly atmosphere. Enjoy the authentic Irish experience with regular entertainment, a wide selection of drinks, and a dog-friendly environment.

-> H91 KN88. Wheelchair Accessible. Dog-friendly. ///relying.trifles.scraped

Royal Garden Chinese Carraroe
Carraroe Chinese Restaurant, also known as Royal Villa, offers a delightful blend of European and Oriental cuisine in the beautiful village of Carraroe in Co Galway. Open seven days a week, their menu caters to a variety of tastes, making it a go-to destination for an enjoyable dining experience.

-> H91 NA7N. ///stow.infiltrate.bouquet

The Quays Bar and Restaurant
Located in the heart of Galway's vibrant 'Latin Quarter,' is a renowned music drinking establishment with a history dating back nearly 400 years. Awarded Ireland's Best Live Entertainment Bar in 2022, it offers a lively atmosphere, exceptional live music, and operates from morning until late at night.

->H91 H2RC. Wheelchair Accessible.
///assets.tone.focal

Finnegans
Finnegans in Galway is a charming restaurant offering a cosy atmosphere and a menu that highlights Irish cuisine. Guests rave about the perfectly cooked soup, shepherd's pie, and bacon. Indulge in delicious desserts like apple pie and cheesecake. With friendly staff and fair prices, Finnegans is a must-visit spot in Galway.

-> H91 E8N5. ///hulk.rescue.farms

Where to Stay
in Connemara

Hotels
- Ballynahinch Castle (Wheelchair Accessible)
- Ardagh Hotel & Restaurant
- Ben Lettery Connemara Hostel
- Murlach Lodge
- Cashel House Hotel
- The Snug Townhouse
- Sleepzone Galway City Hostel (Wheelchair accessible)

Self-Catering Apartments
- Half Acre Cottage
- Emlaghmore Cottage
- Knockbroughaun Cottage
- Galway Coast Cottages
- Dunaras Self Catering
- Menlo Park Self Catering

Campsites

Spiddal Caravan & Camping
Ideally situated on the banks of the Boluisce River, near the Aran Islands and Galway city. With 18 hardstands and ample camping areas, the park offers electricity, water supply, and excellent amenities including toilets, showers, laundry, and a play area.

-> H91 RP80. Dog-friendly.
///thankfully.spouses.handfuls

Salthill Caravan Camping
Salthill Caravan Park, a popular destination for over 50 years, earns a distinguished reputation for cleanliness and comfort. With breathtaking views of Galway Bay on three sides and easy access to the strand, the park offers convenience and natural beauty. The abundance of facilities, including a 24-hour Campers Kitchen, ensures a comfortable stay for all guests.

-> H91 E9C3. Dog-friendly. ///cracks.dare.flag

74 DOG'S BAY

Roadtrip Essentials
in Connemara

Food Shops
- Keoghs MACE Ballyconneely
- Leavys
- Spar
- Tesco Express
- McNamaras
- Aldi, Galway
- Tesco, Galway

Water Points and CDP
- Ballyconneely High Street (Water Only)
- Roundstone Pier (Water Only)
- Cashel Co Aire (Water and CDP)
- Oughterard (Water Only)
- Spiddal Pier (Water Only)

Electric Vehicle Charging Points
- EVBox Charging Station, Connemara NP visitor Centre ///undermines.fulfilling.undulation
- VIRTA Charging Station, Killeen ///rant.healing.ability
- Electric Vehicle Charging Station, The Twelve Hotel ///lotteries.dines.forwarding
- PitPoint Charging Station: Q-Park Eyre Square ///dark.truly.vast

74 DOG'S BAY

Burren and West Clare

In the mystical realm of Burren and West Clare, you will begin to feel as though you have been transported to another world. It is here that you are met with a karst landscape and rolling hills with limestone pavements, earning their Irish name 'An Bhoireann', meaning rock.

In this land of contrasts, the Burren's limestone pavements and the emerald meadows of West Clare stand testament to the eternal struggle between the elements, each carving their own unique tapestry across the landscape. Here, the echoes of bygone eras linger in the air, as the spirits of ancient chieftains and mythical creatures weave their tales amidst the windswept hills and the haunting beauty of the Cliffs of Moher.

The Burren and West Clare region of Ireland offers a plethora of unique attractions and experiences for visitors to explore. One of the most iconic sights in the area is the Cliffs of Moher, where astonishing sea cliffs stretch for 14kms along the Atlantic coast, reaching heights of up to 214m. There is a great visitor centre here where you can learn more about this incredible coastline.

A visit to the Burren National Park provides an opportunity to discover the region's distinctive limestone pavement, rare flora, and fascinating archaeological sites, such as the Poulnabrone Dolmen. In West Clare, the charming village of Doolin serves as a gateway to the Aran Islands and is renowned for its traditional Irish music sessions in local pubs. The Loop Head Peninsula, with its stunning coastal scenery and historic lighthouse, offers a captivating blend of natural beauty and cultural heritage.

For those interested in marine life, dolphin-watching boat trips in the Shannon Estuary provide an unforgettable experience. Additionally, the region boasts a rich culinary scene, with local seafood and farm-to-table dining options that showcase the best of Irish cuisine. With its diverse attractions and activities, the Burren and West Clare region promises a truly memorable and enriching visit for travellers seeking to explore the heart of Ireland's magical landscape.

In order to reach this region, the closest airport is at Craughwell Airport to the east of Galway. You can also reach this area easily by public transport, transiting to Gort by train and then changing to the local bus service. You can also rent a car from here and drive out to the coastline.

79. Dunguaire Castle

Perched elegantly on the tranquil shores of Galway Bay, the captivating 16th-century tower house known as Dunguaire Castle weaves a spellbinding tale of history and charm. With its alluring architecture and stunning backdrop, this enchanting fortress has inspired countless artists and writers, such as W.B. Yeats and Lady Gregory, who often gathered here during the Celtic Revival movement.

It is possible to book a table for dinner in this castle, where you can enjoy an extravagant meal surrounded by the ancient history of the castle walls.

-> *Take the N67 road south towards Kinvara for 25kms, and the castle will appear on the right before entering the village. Wheelchair accessible. ///dryly.genetic.witchcraft.*

79 DUNGUAIRE CASTLE

80. Corcomroe Abbey

Amidst the rugged beauty of County Clare's Burren region, the haunting ruins of a 12th-century Cistercian monastery beckon visitors to explore its rich history and architectural splendour. Known as Corcomroe Abbey, this sacred site enchants with its ornate carvings and a serene atmosphere that whispers tales of the past. The surrounding landscape, home to the Burren's renowned limestone pavements and rare wildflowers, adds to the Abbey's mystical charm. Intriguingly, the Abbey's founder, King Conor na Siudane Ua Briain, is buried here, making it a unique royal resting place.

-> Travel from Ballyvaughan along the R480 road heading south for 9kms, and the Abbey will be on your left. Wheelchair accessible. Dog-friendly. ///gargle.fluency.seashells

81. Burren
A breathtaking landscape unfolds in County Clare, Ireland, where the mesmerising Burren region captivates with its striking limestone pavements, rare flora, and ancient monuments. This geological wonder, formed over 350 million years ago, offers a rich tapestry of history, nature, and culture for visitors to explore. Interestingly, the Burren hosts over 70% of Ireland's native plant species, making it a haven for botanists and nature enthusiasts alike.

-> Take the N67 road south towards Ballyvaughan for approximately 48kms, and the region will be on your right. Some accessible walking trails and visitor centres are available, such as the Burren National Park's Knockaunroe Turlough Trail. Dog-friendly. ///sanity.pose.turmoil

82. Flaggy Shore
Stretching along the northern coast of County Clare, the captivating Flaggy Shore offers a stunning fusion of land and sea, where rugged limestone meets the wild Atlantic waves. This scenic coastal pathway, immortalized in Seamus Heaney's poem "Postscript," invites visitors to marvel at the diverse array of flora and fauna thriving in this unique ecosystem. The Flaggy Shore is also part of the UNESCO-recognized Burren and Cliffs of Moher Geopark, highlighting its geological significance.

-> Drive from Ballyvaughan on the R477 road heading east for 8kms, and the shoreline will be on your right. Wheelchair accessible. Dog-friendly. ///abbeys.doorknobs.princesses

83. Muckinish West Tower House
Standing sentinel along the picturesque shores of Galway Bay, the enigmatic ruins of Muckinish West Tower House evoke tales of a bygone era. This 16th-century fortress, once a stronghold of the O'Loghlen clan, now serves as a striking landmark amidst the rugged beauty of the Burren region.

Interestingly, Muckinish West Tower House is one of several tower houses scattered throughout the area, showcasing the region's rich architectural and historical heritage.

-> Take the R477 road heading west for 12kms, then turn right onto the L1014 road and follow it for 3.5kms. ///harvester.swooned.harps

82 FLAGGY SHORE

85 FANORE BEACH

84. Ballyvaughan

Nestled along the southern shores of Galway Bay, the charming village of Ballyvaughan serves as a gateway to the enchanting Burren region. This picturesque haven, with its colorful houses and welcoming atmosphere, offers visitors a delightful blend of Irish culture, history, and natural beauty. Ballyvaughan boasts a rich artistic heritage, as evidenced by its vibrant community of artists and craftspeople. The village was once a thriving port, with limestone and seaweed exported to Britain in the 19th century.

-> Take the N67 road south for approximately 48 kilometers, and the village will be on your left. Wheelchair accessible. Dog-friendly.
///dripped.voluptuous.antlers

85. Fanore Beach

Golden sands embrace the rugged coastline of County Clare at the stunning Fanore Beach, where the untamed beauty of the Atlantic Ocean meets the unique landscape of the Burren. This Blue Flag beach is a haven for surfers, swimmers, and nature lovers alike, with its pristine waters and captivating views. Notably, the beach lies within the Burren and Cliffs of Moher Geopark, a UNESCO Global Geopark, showcasing the region's geological and ecological significance.

-> Follow the R477 road west for 16kms, and the beach will be on your right. Wheelchair accessible. Dog-friendly.
///catapult.speechless.wham

86. Inisheer

A gem in the heart of the Atlantic, Inisheer is the smallest of the Aran Islands, radiating with Irish charm and breathtaking landscapes. This enchanting isle captivates visitors with its ancient stone forts, sunken shipwrecks, and miles of unspoiled beaches. Home to just 260 residents, Inisheer boasts a tight-knit community that preserves the Irish language and traditional customs.

The island's limestone terrain is home to over 500 varieties of wildflowers, which looks beautiful when they are all in bloom.

-> Take a ferry from Doolin or Rossaveel, or opt for a short flight from Connemara Airport. Wheelchair accessible. Dog-friendly. ///briefing.slouching.surroundings

87. Inishmore

Steeped in history and natural beauty, Inishmore is the largest of the Aran Islands, offering a treasure trove of ancient monuments, dramatic cliffs, and pristine beaches. This captivating haven is renowned for its iconic prehistoric fort, Dún Aonghasa, perched dramatically on the edge of a 100-meter cliff.

With over 50 ancient monuments scattered across the island, Inishmore is a testament to Ireland's rich heritage. A lesser-known fact is that the island is home to the world's smallest church, the Temple Benan, measuring just 11 feet by 7 feet.

-> Take a ferry from Rossaveel or Doolin, or a short flight from Connemara Airport. Wheelchair accessible. Dog-friendly. ///arctic.subjects.toys

88. Cliffs of Moher

Soaring majestically above the wild Atlantic Ocean, the breathtaking Cliffs of Moher stretch for eight kilometers along the coast of County Clare, reaching heights of up to 214 meters. These dramatic cliffs, formed over 300 million years ago, are home to a diverse array of seabirds.

As one of Ireland's most popular tourist attractions, the Cliffs of Moher offer magical views and a captivating glimpse into the country's geological history. A lesser-known fact is that the cliffs have featured in several films, including the iconic 1987 movie "The Princess Bride" as well as "Harry Potter and the Half Blood Prince."

-> Follow the R478 road north for 5kms, and the visitor center will be on your left. Wheelchair accessible. Dog-friendly. ///resonates.legislation.speared

89. Lahinch

A vibrant coastal town on the edge of the Atlantic, Lahinch boasts a stunning stretch of golden sand and rolling surf, making it a popular destination for beachgoers and surf enthusiasts alike. This lively town offers a delightful mix of traditional Irish charm, with its bustling streets lined with pubs, restaurants, and shops.

If you love golf, you will be thrilled to know that Lahinch is home to a world-renowned golf course, attracting players from around the globe with its challenging links and breathtaking scenery.

-> Follow the N67 road southwest for 3kms, and the town will be on your right. Wheelchair accessible. During the Summer, dogs are not allowed on the main beach between 11 am and 6 pm.

Where to Eat
in Burren and West Clare

Hazel Mountain Chocolate
From hand-painted truffles to vegan and Irish milk chocolate creations, their delectable treats have earned them a spot as one of the top food destinations in Ireland. If that's not enough, their award-winning hot chocolate will warm your heart and soul.
-> H91V CF1. *Wheelchair Accessible.*
///fillings.frontal.crammed

Monks Ballyvaughan
With a wide range of dishes and a cosy atmosphere, this restaurant offers a taste of Ireland. From freshly prepared seafood to traditional Irish stew, Monks delivers a memorable dining experience. Top-class service and a friendly staff complete the picture.
-> H91 W9TN. *Wheelchair Accessible.*
///heavily.forefront.forefinger

The Larder, Ballyvaughan
The Larder in Ballyvaughan is highly recommended for tasty and affordable food. With a cosy ambiance and friendly staff, it's the perfect spot for breakfast, lunch or any meal in-between. Vegetarian options are available and delicious desserts including brownies are a must-try.
-> H91 W8WH. ///narrates.figures.belonged

Anthony's at Doolin Inn
Indulge in authentic Irish cuisine at Anthony's, located inside the cosy and modern Doolin Inn. With a focus on sustainability and local ingredients, every dish brings the unique flavors of the Burren to your table. Accompanied by daily live music, this restaurant creates a truly memorable dining experience.
-> V95 CC79. *Wheelchair Accessible.*
///consonant.roasting.conquests

The Hungry Veggie
Experience a culinary journey filled with nourishing and delicious vegetarian options. From savory entrees to indulgent desserts, all with the breathtaking views of the Cliffs of Moher. The Hungry Veggie has something for everyone seeking a vegetarian dining experience.
-> V95 XK00. *Wheelchair Accessible. Dog-friendly* ///crystals.payrolls.alloys

Raviolo Verde
From the comforting aroma of homemade pasta to the perfectly crafted wood-fired pizzas, every bite feels like a taste of la dolce vita. With an intimate and vibrant ambiance, this ristorante and pizzeria transports you straight to the streets of Italy. Highly recommended.
-> V95 AW8C. *Wheelchair Accessible.*
///readymade.seethed.validation

Where to Stay
in Burren and West Clare

Hotels
- Fallons Bed & Breakfast
- Hylands Burren Hotel (Dog-friendly)
- The Waters Country House
- Seacoast Lodge
- The Sleepy Leprechaun (Wheelchair Accessible)
- The Lodges @ Sea View House Doolin
- Cliffs Of Moher Hotel
- Lahinch Coast Hotel

Self-Catering Apartments
- Into The Burren
- Rays Country Cottages (Wheelchair Accessible)
- The Lodge Doolin (Wheelchair Accessible)
- Fanore Self Catering
- Castle View Rooms (Dog-friendly)
- Klondell House Lahinch

Campsites

Nagles Camping & Caravan Park
Located near Doolin Pier and the Cliffs of Moher, the site offers stunning views and top-notch facilities including a playground, showers, laundry, and a grocery store. It offers pitches for touring vans, motorhomes, and tents, with all of the facilities that you need for a comfortable stay, including a newly built playpark.
-> V95 HX25. Wheelchair Accessible. Dog-friendly. ///fielder.host.sweated

O'Connor's Riverside Park
O'Connor's Camping Doolin is a fantastic camping site centrally located in the village of Doolin. The campground is conveniently situated within walking distance of pubs, shops, and various attractions including trips to the Aran Islands, coastal walks, caves, pony trekking, and more.
-> V95 KP99. Wheelchair Accessible. Dog-friendly. ///crystals.payrolls.alleys

RUA Camping Inis Oírr
RUA Camping on Inis Oirr offers spacious tents and bell tents on the smallest of the Aran Islands. Easily accessible by boat from Doolin, this campsite offers breathtaking views of the western coast of Co. Clare. With a perfect location just a short walk from the island's pier, you can start your adventure in no time.
-> H91 YN47. ///grinned.fire.dissonance

84 BALLYVAUGHAN

Roadtrip Essentials
in Burren and West Clare

Food Shops
- Londis Clarinbridge
- Centra Kilcolgan
- Spar, Ballyvaughan
- MACE Lisdoonvarna
- Spar Lahinch

Water Points
- Circle K, Kilcolgan (Water Only)
- Top Garage, Kilcolgan (Water Only)
- BallyVaughan Port (Water Only)
- Main Street Tap, Fanore (Water Only)

Electric Vehicle Charging Points
- Tesla Destintation Charger, The Merriman Hotel Bar & Restaurant, Dungory West /// coated.informer.cape
- ESB Charging Station, 2 Station Rd, Gort /// limiting.kingpin.recover
- be.ENERGISED Charging Station, Monks Ballyvaughan, Lisnanard ////layers.cost.equestrian
- Tesla Destination Charger, Gregans Castle Hotel, Ballyvaughan: ///gravest.breather.nosh
- ecars Charge Point, Hydro Hotel, Rathbaun ///booths.disrespect.monthly
- ESB Charging Station, Miltown Malbay Road ///opera.campaigning.grump
- EVBox Charging Station, Dough, Lahinch /// thermometer.ocean.devote

80 CORCOMROE ABBEY

79 DUNGUAIRE CASTLE

The Shannon Estuary

In the embrace of the majestic River Shannon, the estuary's waters weave a tapestry of life and history, where the river's journey meets the vast expanse of the Atlantic Ocean. The estuary serves as the boundary line separating County Kerry and County Limerick to the south from County Clare to the north.

The length of The Shannon Estuary is 102.1km and it is also known to have a high tidal range. There is a 20 minute ferry that travels across the width of the estuary taking passengers and their vehicles between County Clare and Country Kerry.

As the sun dips below the horizon in the evening, the estuary's waters are set ablaze with hues of gold and crimson, casting a magical glow upon the surrounding landscape. Here, the air is filled with the cries of seabirds and the lapping of waves against the shore, weaving a symphony of nature's harmony. Dolphins are also commonly spotted leaping out of the water in this area.

In order to reach this region, the closest airport is in Shannon to the west of Limerick. You can also reach this area easily by catching the train to Erris, Limerick, or Tralee and then changing to the local bus service. You can also rent a car from here and drive out to the coastline.

90 KILKEE CLIFFS

The Shannon Estuary, located on the west coast of Ireland, is a large tidal estuary where the River Shannon meets the Atlantic Ocean. It offers a variety of attractions and activities for visitors, showcasing the region's rich history, diverse wildlife, and stunning landscapes.

One of the main attractions in the area is the Shannon Estuary Drive, a scenic driving route that takes visitors along the picturesque coastline, passing through charming villages, historic sites, and breathtaking viewpoints. History enthusiasts can explore the numerous castles and forts dotted along the estuary, such as Bunratty Castle, King John's Castle, and Carrigafoyle Castle, each with its own unique story to tell.

The estuary is also home to a thriving population of bottlenose dolphins, making it a popular destination for dolphin-watching boat tours, which depart from the towns of Kilrush and Carrigaholt. Birdwatchers will delight in the estuary's diverse birdlife, including species such as curlews, oystercatchers, and peregrine falcons.

For those seeking outdoor activities, the Shannon Estuary offers excellent opportunities for fishing, sailing, kayaking, and walking, with numerous trails and guided tours available. With its captivating blend of natural beauty, historic treasures, and exciting activities, the Shannon Estuary is a truly unforgettable destination for all who visit.

91 BRIDGES OF ROSS

90. Kilkee Cliffs

Nestled along the rugged coastline of County Clare, the lesser-known but equally stunning Kilkee Cliffs offer a serene and picturesque alternative to the more crowded Cliffs of Moher. These awe-inspiring cliffs stretch for 13 kilometers, with dramatic drops, hidden coves, and breathtaking views of the Atlantic Ocean. The natural beauty and tranquility of the area make it an ideal destination for those seeking a peaceful escape amidst Ireland's wild and rugged landscape.

-> Follow the R487 road westward, and after approximately 1.5 kilometers, you will arrive at the cliffs. Wheelchair accessible. Dog-friendly. ///distancing.ashamed.spaceship

91. Bridges of Ross

Tucked away on the Loop Head Peninsula in County Clare, the Bridges of Ross is a hidden gem, offering visitors a glimpse of Ireland's rugged beauty and coastal splendour. Once a trio of natural sea arches, only one of these geological wonders remains standing today, its limestone formation gracefully sculpted by the relentless waves of the Atlantic Ocean.

The Bridges of Ross is a prime location for seabird watching, attracting bird enthusiasts from around the world during the migration season. We recommend bringing your binoculars.

-> Take the N67 road from Kilkee to the village of Cross, then follow the R487 road westward towards Loop Head. Wheelchair accessible. Dog-friendly. ///stature.unbleached.published

92. Carrigaholt

A picturesque fishing village nestled along the shores of the Shannon Estuary, Carrigaholt captivates visitors with its colorful houses, historic charm, and stunning coastal views. The village is dominated by the 15th-century Carrigaholt Castle, an impressive tower house that once belonged to the powerful McMahon clan.

Carrigaholt also has a reputation as a prime location for dolphin-watching, with a resident pod of bottlenose dolphins frequenting the estuary's waters.

-> Follow the N67 road to the village of Cross, then take the R487 road westward towards Loop Head, turning right onto the R488 road towards Carrigaholt. Wheelchair accessible. Dog-friendly. ///bickering.smelt.philosophers

93. Inis Cathaigh

Steeped in history and shrouded in mystery, Inis Cathaigh, also known as Scattery Island, lies off the coast of County Clare in the Shannon Estuary. This uninhabited island boasts a wealth of ancient ruins, including a round tower, churches, and the remains of a monastic settlement founded by St. Senan in the 6th century. It was once even the site of a Viking invasion, with the island's strategic location making it a prime target for seafaring raiders.

-> Take a ferry from the town of Kilrush, which operates from April to September, weather permitting. The journey takes 30 minutes. Dog-friendly. ///washout.coasting.underpaid

94. Shannon Estuary

A mesmerising blend of natural beauty and rich history, the Shannon Estuary weaves its way along Ireland's west coast, where the River Shannon meets the Atlantic Ocean. This dynamic tidal estuary is home to an array of wildlife, including a resident pod of bottlenose dolphins, making it a popular destination for wildlife enthusiasts. The Shannon Estuary is also one of Europe's deepest natural harbours, allowing large vessels to navigate its waters with ease.

-> *The huge expanse of water leading from the Atlantic Ocean inland to Limerick. It can be passed either by the coastal route via Limerick, or by the ferry at Killimer to Tarbet. ///bookcase.stays.venture*

95. Carrigafoyle Castle

Imagine standing at the edge of a rugged, windswept peninsula, gazing out over the mighty Atlantic Ocean. In the distance, a towering stone structure emerges from the picturesque landscape, its crumbling walls whispering tales of centuries past. This ancient stronghold, nestled in the heart of County Kerry, is a testament to the resilience and tenacity of its builders.

With a fascinating history that dates back to the 15th century, this once formidable fortress witnessed countless battles and sieges. It's said that during a particularly brutal conflict, the nearby town of Ballylongford provided refuge for ships seeking shelter from the stormy waters of the Shannon Estuary. Today, visitors to this captivating site can explore the castle's remnants and imagine the courage and determination of those who once called it home.

-> *Take the N69 road from Listowel to Tarbert, then turn left onto the R551 road towards Ballylongford. The castle is 6kms from Ballylongford. Wheelchair accessible. Dog-friendly. ///optimists.emptiness.drinkable*

94 SHANNON ESTUARY

96. Bromore Cliffs
Soaring majestically above the Atlantic Ocean, Bromore Cliffs provide a breathtaking panorama of County Kerry's rugged coastline.

These awe-inspiring cliffs, which reach heights of up to 180 meters, are adorned with a tapestry of wildflowers and grasses, creating a haven for seabirds and other wildlife. Bromore Cliffs are home to a rare colony of choughs, an elusive bird species known for its striking red beak and legs.

Choughs can be spotted at Bromore Cliffs throughout the year. These stunning birds are known to inhabit the cliff ledges, along with other fascinating bird species such as falcons, ravens, fulmars, guillemots, cormorants, and rock doves.

-> Follow the R551 road from Ballybunion towards Ballyduff, then turn left onto the L1015 road. The cliffs are 4kms from Ballybunion. Wheelchair accessible. Dog-friendly. ///patrols.loses.roved

97. BALLYBUNION

97. Ballybunion
A charming seaside town on the coast of County Kerry, Ballybunion entices visitors with its pristine sandy beaches, striking cliffs, and world-renowned golf courses. Steeped in history, the town is overlooked by the ruins of Ballybunion Castle, which dates back to the 16th century. Ballybunion was also once a favourite holiday destination of former US President Bill Clinton, who visited the town to play golf on its famous links course.

-> Take the N69 road from Listowel, then turn right onto the R553 road towards Ballybunion. The town is approximately 15 kilometers from Listowel. Wheelchair accessible. Dog-friendly. ///heaps.planed.strike

98. Ballyheigue Beach
Nestled along the picturesque coastline of County Kerry, the idyllic Ballyheigue Beach enchants visitors with its golden sands, azure waters, and stunning views of the surrounding landscape. This Blue Flag beach is the perfect destination for families, sunbathers, and water sports enthusiasts alike.

-> To reach Ballyheigue Beach, take the N69 road from Tralee, then turn left onto the R551 road towards Ballyheigue. The beach is 20kms from Tralee. Wheelchair accessible. Dog-friendly. ///workroom.recruiter.antique

99. Blennerville Windmill

The Blennerville Windmill in Tralee, County Kerry, stands as a proud testament to Ireland's rich agricultural heritage. Nestled on the outskirts of the town, this magnificent 18th-century structure is the largest working windmill in the country, captivating visitors with its fascinating history. The windmill's towering sails, impressive grinding stones, and intricate gears showcase the ingenuity of the past, while its idyllic setting amidst rolling hills and verdant fields offers a picturesque backdrop for reflection.

-> Take the N86 road from Tralee town center, heading west towards Dingle. The windmill is 2kms from Tralee. Wheelchair accessible. Dog-friendly. ///lizard.imparts.fleet

100. Glanageenty Forest

A hidden gem nestled in the heart of County Kerry, Glanageenty Forest offers a serene escape into nature's embrace. With its winding trails meandering through lush woodlands, vibrant wildflowers, and picturesque streams, this enchanting forest is a haven for hikers, birdwatchers, and anyone seeking tranquility away from the hustle and bustle of daily life. One captivating fact about Glanageenty Forest is that it was once the stronghold of the legendary 16th-century Gaelic chieftain, O'Sullivan Beare, who was renowned for his bravery and leadership.

-> Take the N21 road towards Tralee, then turn left onto the R558 road. After about 5kms, turn right onto the L2019 road, and follow the signs for Glanageenty Forest. Dog-friendly. ///tiptoes.morally.buildings

99 BLENNERVILLE WINDMILL

Where to Eat
in The Shannon Estuary

Bellbridge House Hotel
The dining experience at the Bellbridge House Hotel in Spanish Point is described as intimate and friendly. Customers can enjoy a wide variety of locally sourced seafood and a selection of fine wines. The hotel also offers private dining options for special occasions.
->V95 HX22. Wheelchair Accessible. ///banker.occasions.heave

The Quilty Tavern
The Quilty Tavern in Ennis, County Clare, is a charming pub and restaurant offering great food, friendly service, and an amazing ocean view. The staff is attentive and the portions are generous. It's a must-visit spot with delicious meals and a relaxed atmosphere.
-> V95 YEE7. ///testified.careful.legion

The Long Dock
Nestled in Carrigaholt, The Long Dock is a seafood lover's haven. Renowned for its diverse menu of locally sourced fish and shellfish, this eatery combines fresh flavours with a warm, inviting ambiance. Patrons often praise its friendly service, making it a must-visit spot in the Shannon Estuary region.
-> V21 A271. Wheelchair Accessible. ///arises.region.bother

Crotty's Pub and B&B
Located in Kilrush, Crotty's is a genuine slice of Irish tradition. More than just a pub, it offers delectable meals in a setting brimming with authenticity. Live music often fills the air, enhancing the experience of enjoying hearty dishes amidst genuine Irish hospitality.
-> V15 K446. Dog-friendly. Wheelchair Accessible. ///trials.slamming.lipstick

The Pantry
Situated in Kilkee, The Pantry is a café-bakery gem. Renowned for its freshly baked pastries and robust coffee, it's a breakfast and lunch favorite. With a reputation built on quality ingredients and a cosy atmosphere, it's a delightful spot for both locals and tourists.
-> V15 R156. Dog-friendly. Wheelchair Accessible. ///fidgets.peeps.dream

Keane's Bar & Restaurant
In the heart of Kilkee lies Keane's, a blend of traditional Irish and modern culinary artistry. With the Atlantic nearby, its seafood dishes are a standout, offering patrons a taste of the ocean's bounty. The restaurant's ambiance and service further elevate the dining experience.
-> V21 A271. Dog-friendly. Wheelchair Accessible. ///rise.boggles.sidle

88 CLIFFS OF MOHER

Where to Stay
in The Shannon Estuary

Hotels
- The Ashe Hotel (Wheelchair Accessible. Dog-friendly)
- The Grand Hotel (Wheelchair Accessible. Dog-friendly)
- Lahinch Coast Hotel & Suites (Wheelchair Accessible. Dog-friendly)
- Shamrock Inn Hotel (Dog-friendly)
- Lehinch Lodge (Wheelchair Accessible)
- Armada Hotel (Wheelchair Accessible. Dog-friendly)

Self-Catering Apartments
- Klondell House (Dog-friendly)
- Woodview, Ennis
- Shannon Springs Hotel (Wheelchair Accessible)
- The Courtyard Apartments (Dog-friendly)
- 20 Lighthouse Village
- The Willows

Campsites

Ocean View Park
A scenic camping park, just a short 10-minute walk from the vibrant town of Lahinch. Perfectly situated amidst some of the best tourist hotspots in Co Clare, it offers stunning views, including the famous Lahinch Beach and the majestic Cliffs of Moher.

-> V95 T0F9. Dog-friendly. ///lookout.inhabitants.cofounded

Strand Camping
Strand Camping in Doonbeg is a serene and picturesque camping site. It offers guests a tranquil, rejuvenating experience right near the beach, making it an absolute favorite destination among nature and beach lovers alike.

-> *V15 W659. Dog-friendly. ///landowner.bowhead.teasing*

Woodlands Park
Woodlands Park is a 4-star family-friendly Caravan and Camping Park located in Tralee, in the beautiful County of Kerry. The park offers a warm welcome to visitors and is known for its top-notch facilities and serene environment.

-> *V92 RW5W. Dog-friendly. Wheelchair Accessible. ///schools.slows.strays*

98 BALLYHEIGUE BEACH

Roadtrip Essentials
in The Shannon Estuary

Food Shops
- McInerney's Shop, Doonbeg
- MACE Kilkee
- Tesco, Kilrush
- Aldi, Kilrush
- Aldi, Ennis
- Lidl, Ennis

Water Points and CDP
- Kilkee Service Station (Water Only)
- Carrigaholt Pier (Water Only)
- Kilrush Marina (CDP & Water)
- Labasheeda Pier (Water Only)
- Kildysart Quay (CDP & Water)
- Bunratty Castle (Water Only)

Electric Vehicle Charging Points
- "ESB Charging Station, East End, Dough /// partied.bloat.perused
- ESB Charging Station, Tesco Kilrush /// outdone.passes.point
- ecars Charge Point Charging Station, Courthouse Lawn, Listowel ///disservice.peoples.sheepskin
- ESB Charging Station, Garvey's carpark, Matt Talbot ///leans.blanks.weaned
- ecars Charge Point, Tralee Bay Wetlands /// handbook.deep.shift
- ESB Charging Station, Killarney Road, Castleisland ///moonwalk.combos.embrace
- Tesla Supercharger, Curragheha East, Leebrook ///monotonous.decorators.tramps "

91 BRIDGES OF ROSS

SIGHTS

Beaches & Harbours
- 101. Castlegregory Beach
- 102. Fermoyle Strand
- 104. Dooneen Pier
- 106. Smerwich Harbour
- 107. Dunquin
- 109. Coumeenole Beach

Viewpoints
- 103. Brandon Point
- 110. Slea Head

Castles & Historical Sights
- 105. Gallarus Oratory
- 111. Dunbeg Fort
- 113. Minard Castle

Towns
- 112. Dingle

Activities
- 108. Blasket Centre

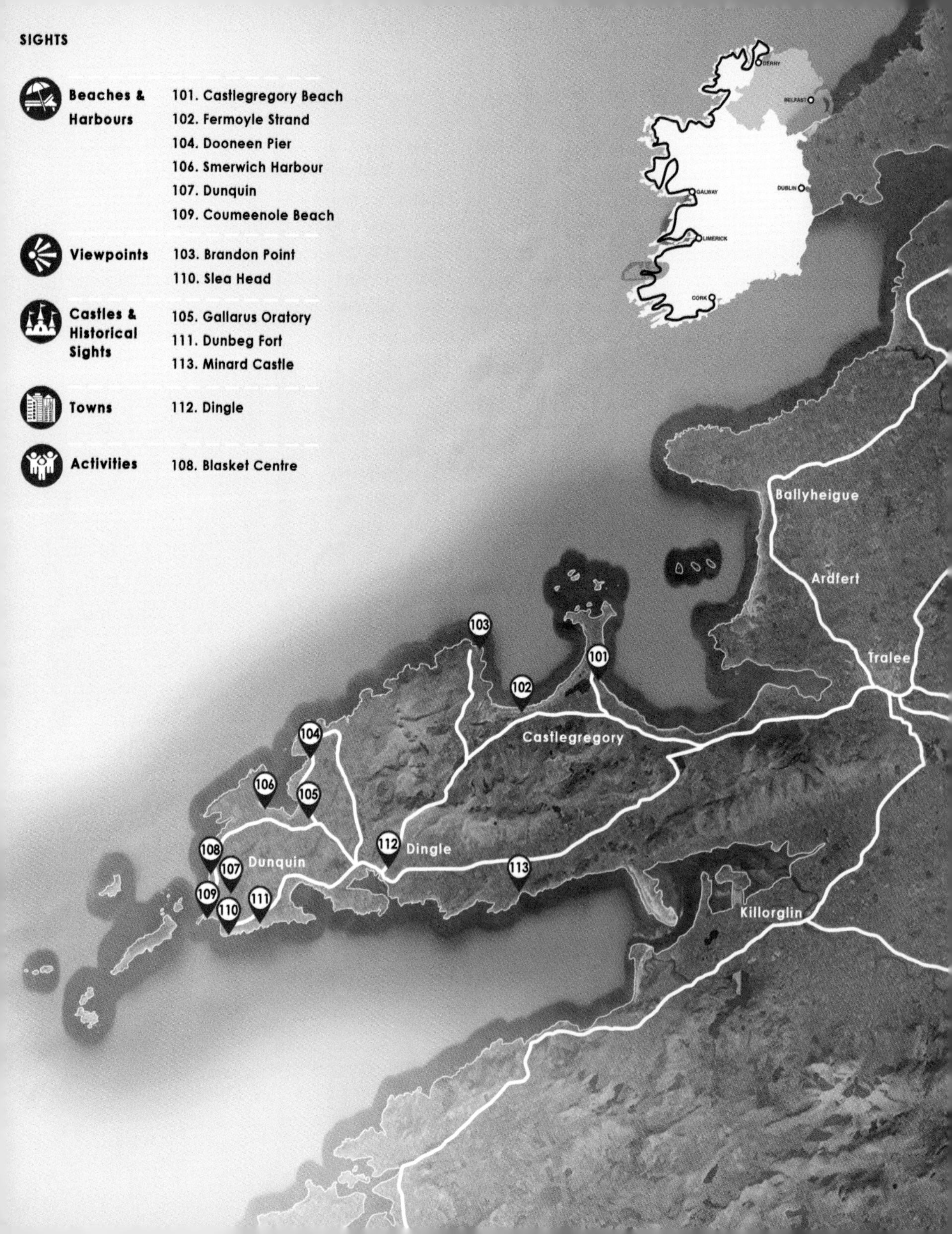

Dingle Peninsula

As the sun rises over the Dingle Peninsula, the world awakens to a symphony of colour and light, casting an ethereal glow upon the rugged landscape. This charming corner of County Kerry is a place where you will no doubt visit and leave wanting to return again and again.

Here, the land meets the sea in a dramatic embrace, as towering cliffs plunge into the wild Atlantic waves below, and the dramatic coatline is dotted with hidden coves of golden sand.

The Dingle Peninsula is a place of contrasts, where the harshness of nature is met with the warmth of human connection. In the charming villages that dot the coastline, the laughter of locals mingles with the lilting melodies of traditional music, creating a true sense of belonging. As you wander the ancient pathways, explore the ruins of forgotten monasteries, or marvel at the wonder of the prehistoric beehive huts, the Dingle Peninsula leaves you with lasting memories.

In order to reach this region, the closest airport is in the Kerry Airport to the east. You can also reach this area easily by catching the train to Tralee, Killarney, or Farranfore and then changing to the local bus service. You can also rent a car from here and drive out to the coastline.

The Dingle Peninsula, located in County Kerry, is a popular destination for travellers seeking a diverse range of attractions and activities. Spanning 48kms in length, the peninsula is home to a variety of natural wonders, historical sites, and charming towns, providing visitors with a wealth of experiences to choose from.

The Slea Head Drive, a scenic route that circumnavigates the peninsula, offers stunning views of the coastline and access to several key attractions, including the Gallarus Oratory, a well-preserved early Christian church, and the Blasket Islands, which can be visited by boat from the village of Dunquin. **NOTE** - *Slea Head Drive must be travelled clockwise due to road restrictions.*

Outdoor enthusiasts will find no shortage of opportunities for hiking, cycling, and water sports on the Dingle Peninsula. The challenging Mount Brandon, Ireland's second-highest peak, rewards climbers with panoramic views, while the more leisurely Dingle Way walking trail meanders through picturesque landscapes and quaint villages.

The town of Dingle itself is a bustling hub of culture and entertainment, featuring a vibrant arts scene, traditional music sessions in local pubs, and a wide array of dining options, including fresh seafood caught daily in the harbour. With its unique blend of natural beauty, rich history, and warm hospitality, the Dingle Peninsula is a must-visit destination for any traveller exploring the Emerald Isle.

108 BLASKET CENTRE

107 DUNQUIN

101. Castlegregory Beach

Nestled between the stunning Dingle Peninsula and the rugged coastline of County Kerry, a hidden gem awaits discovery: the pristine shores of Castlegregory Beach. This expansive stretch of golden sand, lapped by crystal-clear waters, offers an idyllic setting for a leisurely stroll, a refreshing swim, or a fun-filled day with the family.

As the sun sets, painting the sky in hues of pink and orange, the beach becomes a tranquil haven for reflection and relaxation. This picturesque location is also home to a thriving surfing community, thanks to the consistent Atlantic waves that grace its shores.

-> Follow the N86 road from Tralee to Dingle, then take the R560 road towards Castlegregory village. Upon entering the village, follow the signs to the beach, which is located 3kms from the village center. Wheelchair accessible. Dog-friendly. ///candy.napkin.illogical

102. Fermoyle Strand

A breathtaking expanse of golden sand stretches as far as the eye can see, inviting visitors to explore the captivating beauty of Fermoyle Strand. Located on the northern side of the Dingle Peninsula, this magnificent beach is a haven for nature lovers, offering a serene escape from the hustle and bustle of daily life.

The pristine shoreline, caressed by the gentle waves as it sits sheltered from the the Atlantic Ocean, is the perfect setting for a leisurely walk, a refreshing swim, or an invigorating surf session. One fascinating fact about Fermoyle Strand is that it is one of the longest beaches in Ireland, extending over 12 kilometers in length.

-> Take the N86 road from Tralee to Dingle, then turn onto the R560 towards Cloghane. Continue on the R560 until you reach a junction, and follow the sign for Fermoyle Strand. The beach is approximately 5kms from this junction. Dog-friendly. ///unscathed.converters.mirage

103. Brandon Point

Perched on the edge of the Dingle Peninsula, where the land meets the wild Atlantic Ocean, lies the awe-inspiring Brandon Point. This dramatic vantage point offers unparalleled views of the surrounding coastline, the nearby Mount Brandon, and the distant Blasket Islands. As the salty sea breeze caresses your face, you can't help but feel a sense of exhilaration and wonder at the sheer beauty of nature. This breathtaking location lies along the ancient pilgrimage route to the summit of Mount Brandon, a sacred site for Irish Christians since the early medieval period.

-> Follow the N86 road from Tralee to Dingle, then turn onto the R560 towards Cloghane. Continue through Cloghane village, following the signs for Brandon Point. The journey from Cloghane to Brandon Point is 6kms. Wheelchair accessible. Dog-friendly. ///crafty.vase.wader

104. Dooneen Pier

Tucked away on the southern coast of the Dingle Peninsula, a quaint and charming haven awaits exploration: Dooneen Pier. This picturesque spot, with its crystal-clear waters and vibrant marine life, is a favourite among locals for fishing, swimming, and launching small boats.

The tranquil atmosphere is further enhanced by the presence of a historic lime kiln, a testament to the area's rich industrial heritage dating back to the 19th century. As you soak in the serene beauty of Dooneen Pier, it's easy to see why this hidden gem has captured the hearts of those who venture off the beaten path.

-> *Follow the N86 road from Tralee to Dingle, then turn onto the R559 towards Slea Head Drive. Continue on the R559 for 6kms, then turn left at the sign for Dooneen Pier. Dog-friendly. ///gazebo.scorpion.alliances*

105. Gallarus Oratory

Steeped in history and shrouded in mystery, this remarkable architectural gem stands proudly amidst the rolling hills of the Dingle Peninsula. This early Christian church, built between the 6th and 9th centuries, is an exquisite example of drystone construction, with its corbel-vaulted roof remaining remarkably intact to this day.

The oratory's boat-shaped design, resembling an upturned vessel, has led to various interpretations of its symbolic meaning, adding to its allure and fascination for visitors from around the world.

-> *Follow the N86 road from Tralee to Dingle, then take the R559 towards Slea Head Drive. Look for signs directing you to Gallarus Oratory, which is located 6kms off the main road. Dog-friendly. ///procured.treble.spearmint*

105 GALLARUS ORATORY

106. Smerwich Harbour

Nestled along the rugged coastline of the Dingle Peninsula, a picturesque and serene haven awaits. This sheltered bay, with its crystal-clear waters and breathtaking views, offers a perfect setting for a myriad of water-based activities, from sailing and kayaking to fishing and swimming.

Rich in history, Smerwich Harbour was the site of a significant naval battle in 1580 between English forces and a group of Irish and Spanish soldiers, known as the Siege of Smerwick. Today, the tranquil beauty of the harbour belies its tumultuous past, providing a peaceful retreat for those seeking solace by the sea.

-> Follow the N86 from Tralee to Dingle, then take the R559 towards Slea Head Drive. Continue on the R559 for 10kms, then turn left at the sign for Smerwick Harbour. Dog-friendly. ///turmoil.adventure.snack

107. Dunquin

At the westernmost tip of the Dingle Peninsula lies the enchanting village of Dunquin, a captivating blend of breathtaking landscapes and rich cultural heritage. This picturesque settlement, with its traditional Irish cottages and dramatic cliffside views, is the gateway to the Blasket Islands, a group of islands steeped in history and literary tradition.

Dunquin's unique charm is further enhanced by its status as the most westerly settlement in mainland Ireland, offering visitors an unparalleled sense of remoteness and tranquility as they gaze out across the vast expanse of the Atlantic Ocean.

-> Follow the N86 from Tralee to Dingle, then take the R559 towards Slea Head Drive. Continue on the R559 for 20kms, until you reach Dunquin. Wheelchair accessible. Dog-friendly. ///dryly.defied.curable

108. Blasket Centre

Immersed in the rich cultural tapestry of the Dingle Peninsula, a fascinating treasure trove of history and storytelling awaits: the Blasket Centre. This captivating museum, dedicated to preserving the unique heritage of the Blasket Islands, offers a glimpse into the lives of the islanders, who were renowned for their storytelling, music, and literary achievements.

The Centre's exhibits and interactive displays provide a moving tribute to the resilience and creativity of this isolated community, which was evacuated in 1953 due to harsh living conditions and dwindling resources.

-> Follow the N86 road from Tralee to Dingle, then take the R559 towards Slea Head Drive. Continue on the R559 for 20kms, until you reach the sign for the Blasket Centre. Wheelchair accessible. Dog-friendly. ///magician.mixed.speedily

109. Coumeenole Beach

Embraced by the rugged beauty of the Dingle Peninsula, a stunning stretch of golden sand and crystal-clear waters beckons: Coumeenole Beach. This breathtakingly picturesque spot, with its dramatic cliffs and crashing waves, has served as a filming location for the iconic movie "Ryan's Daughter" and the television series "Far and Away." The beach's mesmerising beauty and powerful Atlantic swells make it a popular destination for both sightseers and surfers, providing an unforgettable experience for those who venture to this enchanting corner of Ireland.

-> Follow the N86 to Dingle, then take the R559 towards Slea Head Drive. Continue on the R559 for 22kms, until you reach the sign for Coumeenole Beach. Dog-friendly.
///dancer.fearful.finisher

109 COUMEENOLE BEACH

110 SLEA HEAD

110. Slea Head

Where the wild Atlantic waves meet the rugged Irish coastline, a breathtaking panorama unfolds. This dramatic headland, located on the Dingle Peninsula, offers unparalleled views of the Blasket Islands and the vast expanse of the Atlantic Ocean. It is also home to one of Ireland's most impressive drives, taking visitors clockwise along its winding, clifftop road around the edge of the peninsula. Slea Head is a testament to the untamed beauty of Ireland's western shores. Interestingly, the area is steeped in history, with ancient beehive huts and early Christian sites dotting the landscape, providing a fascinating glimpse into the region's rich past.

-> Follow the N86 to Dingle, then take the R559 towards Slea Head Drive. Continue on the R559 for 24kms, until you reach Slea Head. Wheelchair accessible. Dog-friendly.
///purchase.economically.summer

111. Dunbeg Fort

Perched precariously on a sheer cliff edge along the Dingle Peninsula, an ancient sentinel stands guard known as Dunbeg Fort. This Iron Age promontory fort, dating back to around 500 BC, offers a fascinating insight into the lives of its early inhabitants. With its intricate stone defenses and strategic location, the fort serves as a testament to the ingenuity and resilience of the people who once called this windswept landscape home.

Dunbeg Fort is part of a larger network of forts and archaeological sites that can be found along the peninsula, making it a captivating destination for history enthusiasts.

-> *Follow the N86 to Dingle, then take the R559 towards Slea Head Drive. Continue on the R559 for 8kms, until you reach the sign for Dunbeg Fort. Dog-friendly. ///intense.messing.kinder*

112. Dingle

Nestled along the picturesque coastline of the Dingle Peninsula lies a charming and vibrant town, steeped in history and brimming with Irish culture. Known for its lively pubs, artisan shops, and stunning natural surroundings, Dingle serves as an idyllic base for exploring the wonders of the Wild Atlantic Way.

Interestingly, the town is home to a friendly local celebrity, Fungie the dolphin, who delighted visitors for over three decades with his playful antics in Dingle Harbour, further adding to the town's unique charm and appeal.

-> *Follow the N86 road from Tralee for 50kms, until you arrive in the town. Wheelchair accessible. Dog-friendly. ///revise.twice.secrets*

112 DINGLE

113. Minard Castle

Rising majestically from the rocky shoreline of the Dingle Peninsula, a storied fortress casts its gaze across the wild Atlantic waters. The 16th-century tower house of Minard Castle, built by the Knight of Kerry, stands as a testament to the region's turbulent past and enduring resilience.

Surrounded by a striking storm beach of large boulders, the castle's location offers a dramatic and unforgettable backdrop for visitors seeking to explore Ireland's rich history. Intriguingly, the beach at Minard is one of only three locations in Ireland where these unique geological formations, known as "fossil storm beaches," can be found.

-> *Follow the N86 to Dingle, then take the R560 towards Lispole. Continue on the R560 for 4kms, then turn left onto the L8062 and follow the signs for Minard Castle. Dog-friendly. ///suitcase.neutral.punk*

Where to Eat
in Dingle Peninsula

The Fish Box
Nestled in the heart of Dingle, this establishment is a seafood enthusiast's dream. Fresh Irish seafood takes centre stage, with dishes that capture the essence of the Atlantic. The ambiance is warm and inviting, making it a sought-after spot for both locals and visitors.

-> V92 YC64. ///hiking.poodle.betrayed

Solas Tapas & Wine Bar
This Dingle gem offers a delightful fusion of Irish and Mediterranean flavours. Visitors can indulge in a diverse tapas menu, all while enjoying a curated selection of wines. The setting is chic yet welcoming, perfect for a relaxed evening.

-> V92 A091. ///inches.plea.dads

The Chart House
Positioned as a premium dining destination in Dingle, The Chart House is a haven for seafood aficionados. The sophisticated setting is complemented by a menu that emphasizes quality and freshness, ensuring a dining experience like no other.

-> V92 YA40. ///alright.marker.sailors

Out of the Blue Seafood
Seafood-only restaurant, perfectly situated on the harbour in Dingle. It offers a unique dining experience, focusing on fresh ingredients straight from the ocean. The restaurant is known for its fine, interesting, and colourful dishes, providing a fresh and fun dining experience in a shack-like setting.

-> V92 A6XT. Dog-friendly. ///goats.homework.steroids

Pisces Restaurant
Located in the picturesque Castlegregory, this restaurant is celebrated for its diverse seafood dishes, with a menu that caters to various dietary needs including vegetarian, vegan, and gluten-free options. The ambiance is inviting, making it a preferred choice for both locals and tourists.

-> V92 KN8Y. ///diodes.affair.quietly

Quinn's Pub: The Ventry Inn
Quinn's Pub, also known as The Ventry Inn, has been a family-run establishment since 1971. Located in the heart of Ventry village, it boasts picturesque views overlooking the beach and harbour. The pub serves bar food throughout the day and frequently hosts music sessions, offering a vibrant atmosphere.

-> V92 AW89. ///highway.saucer.cheery

Where to Stay
in Dingle Peninsula

Hotels
- O'Connors Guesthouse
- Dingle Skellig Hotel & Peninsula Spa
- Base Accommodation Dingle
- Barr na Sraide Inn
- Ceann Sibeal Hotel
- Dingle Benners Hotel
- Dingle Bay Hotel (Dog-friendly)
- Milltown House Dingle

Self-Catering Apartments
- Dingle Marina Cottages
- The Dingle Galley
- 6 Gortonora, Dingle (Dog friendly)
- 18 Ard na Mara, Dingle (Wheelchair Accessible)
- An Riasc Farmhouse Rental
- Jacks Country Farmhouse
- Glór na hAbhann Holiday Home, Dingle (Wheelchair Accessible)

Campsites

Green Acres Caravan Park

Located in a fabulous spot right on the beach, Green Acres is the ideal base for exploring the Dingle Peninsula. The campsite offers all the essential facilities, ensuring a comfortable stay. With its pristine surroundings and well-maintained amenities, it's a top choice for campers seeking a blend of nature and convenience.

-> V92 TK40. ///heartbeat.initials.signifying

Campail Teach an Aragail

A family-friendly campsite run with dedication and warmth. The site caters to both young and old, ensuring everyone has a memorable experience. Its strategic location and welcoming atmosphere make it a favourite among visitors to the peninsula.

-> V92 HX95. ///fidgeting.carton.notations

Anchor Caravan Park

Anchor Caravan Park, located in Castlegregory on the Dingle Peninsula, is a picturesque seaside caravan park. It's a preferred destination for those who wish to experience the beauty of the Dingle Peninsula up close. The park is known for its scenic views, well-maintained facilities, and its proximity to the sandy beaches.

-> V92 YD42. Dog-friendly.
///marvel.daffodil.dupe

Roadtrip Essentials
in Dingle Peninsula

Food Shops
- Aldi, Tralee
- Tesco Superstore, Tralee
- Lidl, Tralee
- Spar, Castlegregory
- Lidl, Dingle
- Morans Supermarket, Dingle

Water Points and CDP
- Aughacasla Daybreak (Water Only)
- Bridge Field Aire (Water & CDP)
- Scraggane Bay Harbour (Water Only)
- West Kerry Brewer (Water Only)
- Ventry Bay (Water Only)
- Moran's Garage, Dingle (Water Only)
- Campail Teach an Aragail Campsite (Water & CDP)

Electric Vehicle Charging Points
- "ecars Charge Point, Tralee Bay Wetlands ///handbook.deep.shift
- ESB Charging Station, Texaco, Mail Road, Dingle ///noble.cursing.offer
- ESB Charging Station, Marina Car Park, Dingle ///ripe.stumps.librarian"

107 DUNQUIN

Ring of Kerry

As you set foot upon the mystical lands of the Ring of Kerry, a sense of wonder and enchantment envelops you, whispering the secrets of its ancient past and the timeless beauty that lies within. The lush, verdant hills roll gently towards the horizon, cradling sparkling lakes that mirror the ever-changing Irish skies. The wild Atlantic waves crash against the jagged cliffs, weaving a mesmerising tapestry of power and grace, while the soft, golden sands of hidden beaches beckon you to leave your footprints upon their pristine shores.

Here, in this land of legends and lore, the vibrant hues of wildflowers paint the countryside, and the haunting cries of seabirds echo through the salty air. Amidst the breathtaking panorama, quaint villages and bustling towns spring forth, their brightly coloured cottages and lively pubs radiating warmth and friendliness.

As you wander through this captivating kingdom, let the lilting melodies of traditional Irish music guide your steps, and allow the rich variety of flavours, aromas, and textures to awaken your senses, weaving an unforgettable tale of the Ring of Kerry's enchanting allure.

In order to reach this region, the closest airport is the Kerry Airport to the east. You can also reach this area easily by public transport, by catching the train to Killarney and then changing to the local bus service. You can also rent a car from here and drive out to the coastline.

The Ring of Kerry, a 179-kilometre scenic drive in County Kerry, Ireland, is a treasure trove of natural wonders, historical sites, and cultural gems. As you journey along this iconic route, you'll encounter awe-inspiring landmarks such as the Gap of Dunloe, with its dramatic mountain pass, and the serene beauty of Killarney National Park, home to the magnificent Torc Waterfall and the historic Muckross House and Gardens.

Venture further along the coast to discover the UNESCO World Heritage Site of Skellig Michael, an ancient monastic settlement perched precariously atop a rocky island, and the picturesque towns of Kenmare and Waterville, where you can indulge in the region's renowned culinary delights and vibrant arts scene. Outdoor enthusiasts will relish the opportunity to explore the Ring of Kerry's diverse landscapes, from hiking the rugged peaks of Carrauntoohil and Mount Brandon to surfing the Atlantic swells at Inch Beach.

Throughout the year, the region hosts a plethora of events and festivals, such as the Rose of Tralee International Festival and the Killorglin Puck Fair, offering visitors a unique insight into the rich cultural heritage that defines the Ring of Kerry. With its unparalleled beauty, fascinating history, and warm Irish hospitality, the Ring of Kerry promises an unforgettable adventure that will linger in your heart long after you've left its shores.

114. Caragh Lake

Nestled amidst the majestic mountains and verdant forests of County Kerry, a shimmering oasis of tranquility awaits the discerning traveller. This hidden gem, known as Caragh Lake, captivates the senses with its crystal-clear waters, which mirror the ever-changing hues of the Irish sky. Renowned for its abundant brown trout population, Caragh Lake offers anglers a serene haven to cast their lines and immerse themselves in nature. The idyllic surroundings are the perfect place for a relaxing walk as you listen to the the gentle lapping of the waves and the rustling of leaves around you.

-> Follow the N70 towards Glenbeigh for 7kms, then turn left onto the L4024 road and continue for another 4kms until you reach the lake. Wheelchair accessible. Dog-friendly. ///mutiny.sweaty.listings

115. Dooks Beach

A haven of golden sands and turquoise waters, embraced by the rugged beauty of County Kerry's coastline, beckons those seeking solace in nature's embrace. This serene sanctuary, invites you to leave their footprints upon its pristine shores, while the gentle lapping of waves whispers soothing melodies. Known for its unique and diverse ecosystem, Dooks Beach is home to the rare and protected Natterjack Toad, a fascinating inhabitant that adds an air of intrigue to this picturesque haven. As you stroll along the shore, let the salty sea breeze wash over your skin, and allow the breathtaking scenery to etch an indelible memory upon your heart.

-> Take the N70 towards Glenbeigh and turn off at the sign for Dooks Golf Club. Follow the narrow road for 2kms, until you reach the beach. Wheelchair accessible. Dog-friendly. ///unlucky.limited.gargle

116. Leacanabuaile Ring Fort

Steeped in history and shrouded in mystery, an ancient stronghold stands sentinel over the verdant landscape of County Kerry. This enigmatic site, Leacanabuaile Ring Fort, transports visitors back in time, offering a glimpse into the lives of its inhabitants over a thousand years ago. Dating back to the 9th or 10th century, the fort's remarkably well-preserved stone walls and dwellings provide an intriguing insight into Ireland's rich Celtic past. As you wander through this timeless monument, let the whispers of history guide your imagination, and envision the daily lives of those who once called this mystical place home.

-> Follow the N70 towards Waterville, and turn off at the sign for the fort, located 3kms outside Cahersiveen. Continue for another 2kms, passing the Cahergall Ring Fort, until you reach Leacanabuaile. Wheelchair accessible. Dog-friendly. ///gigantic.valves.taking

115 DOOKS BEACH

117. Valentia Island Lighthouse

Perched on the edge of a rocky promontory, a beacon of light stands tall, guiding mariners through the treacherous waters of the wild Atlantic Ocean. This enduring sentinel, casts a warm glow over the rugged coastline, illuminating the rich history and maritime heritage of its surroundings.

Established in 1841, the lighthouse's iconic white tower and charming keeper's cottage offer a captivating glimpse into the lives of the courageous souls who once tended its vital flame. As you explore this enchanting landmark, let the salty sea breeze and the distant cries of seabirds transport you back in time, immersing you in the captivating tale of Valentia Island Lighthouse.

-> Follow the N70 and take the bridge onto Valentia Island. Continue along the R565 road for 4kms, then turn left at the sign for the lighthouse and follow the narrow road to the entrance. Not Suitable for large vehicles. Wheelchair accessible. Dog-friendly.
///paid.handhelds.cramming.

117 VALENTIA ISLAND LIGHTHOUSE

118. The Valentia Island Tetrapod Footprints

A testament to the passage of time and the inexorable march of evolution, this series of ancient imprints lie etched upon the rocky shores of Valentia Island. These remarkable relics, bear witness to a pivotal moment in Earth's history, when the first creatures emerged from the primordial seas to venture onto land. Dating back around 385 million years, these exceptionally well-preserved tracks offer a fascinating window into a world long vanished, inviting visitors to ponder the extraordinary journey of life on our planet.

-> Follow the N70 and cross the bridge onto Valentia Island. Continue along the R565 road for 3kms, then turn left at the sign for the Tetrapod Trackway and follow the narrow road. Dog-friendly. ///reason.splash.beasts

118 THE VALENTIA ISLAND TETRAPOD FOOTPRINTS

119. Fogher Cliffs (Aillte Fogher)

Rising majestically 180m from the churning waters of the Atlantic, a breathtaking spectacle of sheer rock and untamed beauty captivates the senses. These magnificent formations, Fogher Cliffs (Aillte Fogher), stand as a testament to the relentless power of nature, carving a dramatic silhouette against the ever-changing canvas of the Irish sky. Home to a diverse array of seabirds, including puffins and guillemots, the cliffs provide a sanctuary for these captivating creatures, adding an air of enchantment to this mesmerising landscape.

-> Follow the N70 and cross the bridge onto Valentia Island. Continue along the R565 road for 5kms, then turn left at the sign for Bray Head and follow to the parking area. Dog-friendly. ///sticking.contingent.bandit

119 FOGHER CLIFFS (AILLTE FOGHER)

120. Portmagee

Nestled along the rugged coastline of County Kerry, a charming fishing village beckons with its colourful houses and warm Irish hospitality. This picturesque haven, serves as a gateway to the enchanting Skellig Islands, inviting visitors to embark on an unforgettable journey across the wild Atlantic.

Steeped in maritime history and named after a legendary 18th-century smuggler, Captain Theobald Magee, the village offers a delightful blend of culture, heritage, and natural beauty. As you meander through its quaint streets, let the gentle lilt of traditional music and the irresistible aroma of freshly caught seafood tempt you to linger a while in this captivating corner of the Emerald Isle.

-> Follow the N70 and take the turnoff towards the village, which is well signposted. Wheelchair accessible. Dog-friendly. ///likens.goalie.since

122. Puffin Island

A haven for seabirds and a jewel in the crown of the Ring of Kerry, an enchanting isle lies just off the coast of County Kerry. Puffin Island, as its name suggests, is home to a thriving colony of these endearing birds, their distinctive beaks and vibrant plumage adding a touch of magic to the rugged landscape.

In addition to puffins, the island hosts numerous other seabird species, including razorbills and guillemots, creating a bustling symphony of life amidst the wild beauty of the Atlantic.

-> Head to the nearby Kerry Cliffs or Valentia Island, both of which offer stunning views of the island from their vantage points. Alternatively, boat tours from Portmagee often include a trip around Puffin Island. Wheelchair accessible viewpoints. Dog-friendly viewpoints. ///faraway.sharing.pavilions

121. Kerry Cliffs (Aillte Chiarraí)

Soaring high above the crashing waves of the Atlantic Ocean, a breathtaking panorama unfolds before your eyes. These incredible natural wonders, Kerry Cliffs (Aillte Chiarraí), offer unparalleled views of the iconic Skellig Islands and the distant Puffin Island, where seabirds nest in their thousands. Formed over 400 million years ago, the cliffs stand as a testament to the unyielding forces of nature, carving a dramatic landscape that captivates the hearts and minds of all who visit.

-> Follow the N70 from Portmagee for 3kms, then turn off at the sign for the cliffs and continue to the parking area. Wheelchair accessible. Dog-friendly. ///scuba.drab.spatial

121 KERRY CLIFFS (AILLTE CHIARRAÍ)

123. Ballinskelligs Bay

Embraced by the rugged beauty of the Iveragh Peninsula, a crescent of golden sand and azure waters beckons visitors to a tranquil haven. Ballinskelligs Bay, with its pristine shoreline and gentle waves, offers a serene escape from the bustling world beyond. Steeped in history, the bay is overlooked by the haunting ruins of Ballinskelligs Castle, a 16th-century tower house that stands sentinel over the surrounding landscape. As you stroll along the sands, let the whispers of the past and the soothing rhythm of the ocean lull you into a state of blissful reverie.

-> *Follow the N70 then take the R567 towards Ballinskelligs. The bay is well signposted and easily accessible by car. Wheelchair accessible. Dog-friendly. ///lengthen.skid.glossy*

124. Loher Stone Fort

Whispers of ancient battles and long-forgotten tales echo through the walls of a remarkable structure nestled amidst the rolling hills of County Kerry. This impressive monument stands as a testament to Ireland's rich past, its circular stone walls providing a glimpse into the lives of those who once called this place home.

Dating back to the 9th century, the fort was once a defensive stronghold and a symbol of power for the chieftains who ruled the land. As you wander through the ruins, let your imagination transport you to a time of warriors, feasts, and the enduring spirit of the Irish people.

-> *Follow the N70 then take the R567 towards Ballinskelligs. Turn off at the sign for Loher Stone Fort and continue along the narrow road to the parking area. Dog-friendly. ///raged.melon.cheekbones*

125. Abbey Island

Steeped in history and surrounded by the wild beauty of the Atlantic Ocean, a small, windswept isle beckons to those seeking a glimpse into Ireland's storied past. Abbey Island, so named for the ruins of the 8th-century Derrynane Abbey that lie upon its shores, offers a hauntingly beautiful landscape where the echoes of monks' chants and the whispers of ancient prayers intertwine with the song of the sea.

As you explore the island's rugged shoreline and crumbling walls, let the serenity of this sacred place envelop you, transporting you to a time when spirituality and nature were inextricably intertwined.

-> Follow the N70 then take the R566 towards Derrynane. Follow the signs for Derrynane Beach and park in the designated parking area. A short walk across the beach at low tide will bring you to Abbey Island. Dog-friendly. ///pursued.parts.windmills

125 ABBEY ISLAND

126. Derrynane Beach & Darrynane Beg Ogham Stone

Nestled along the picturesque coastline of County Kerry, a stunning expanse of golden sands and gentle waves invites visitors to bask in the beauty of the Emerald Isle. Derrynane Beach, with its crystal-clear waters and breathtaking views, is a true gem of the Ring of Kerry. Just a short distance away, the ancient Darrynane Beg Ogham Stone stands in silent testimony to Ireland's rich Celtic heritage.

Inscribed with the earliest form of the Irish language, this enigmatic monument offers a tangible connection to the island's distant past, its weathered markings a testament to the resilience of a culture that has endured for centuries.

-> Follow the N70 then take the R566 towards Derrynane. Follow the signs for Derrynane Beach and park in the designated parking area. Derrynane Beach is wheelchair accessible, ,however, the Ogham Stone may not be. Dog-friendly. ///mayhem.proclaimed.restriction

126 DERRYNANE BEACH & DARRYNANE BEG OGHAM

127. Staigue Stone Fort

Amidst the rugged landscape of County Kerry, a remarkable feat of ancient engineering stands as a testament to the ingenuity and resilience of the Irish people.

Staigue Stone Fort, with its massive dry-stone walls and intricate construction, offers a fascinating glimpse into the lives of those who inhabited this remote corner of the world over a thousand years ago. As you explore the fort's winding passages and marvel at the skill and craftsmanship that went into its creation, let the spirit of the past envelop you, transporting you to a time when warriors and chieftains roamed the land.

-> Follow the N70 then take the R568 towards Castlecove. Turn off at the sign for Staigue Stone Fort and continue along the narrow road to the parking area. Dog-friendly. ///sheltered.lasers.relaxing

128. Moll's Gap

High in the mountains of County Kerry, a breathtaking vista unfolds before your eyes, revealing the awe-inspiring beauty of the Irish landscape. Moll's Gap, a panoramic viewpoint along the Ring of Kerry, captivates visitors with its sweeping views of the MacGillycuddy's Reeks and the surrounding countryside.

As you stand amidst the rugged terrain, enveloped in the crisp mountain air, let the stunning scenery inspire a sense of wonder and appreciation for the majesty of nature. Interestingly, Moll's Gap is named after Moll Kissane, who ran a small shebeen (unlicensed drinking establishment) in the area during the 19th century.

-> Follow the N71 from either Kenmare or Killarney. The viewpoint is located halfway between these two towns and is easily accessible from the main road. Wheelchair accessible. Dog-friendly. ///easiest.weep.devoid

128 MOLL'S GAP

129. Gap of Dunloe

Carved by glaciers eons ago, a narrow mountain pass in County Kerry invites intrepid explorers to embark on an unforgettable journey through the heart of the Irish countryside. The Gap of Dunloe, with its rugged cliffs, sparkling lakes, and verdant valleys, offers a truly mesmerising experience as you traverse its winding trails. As you immerse yourself in the serene beauty of this enchanting landscape, you may encounter the famous Wishing Bridge, where legend has it that wishes made while crossing are destined to come true.

-> Follow the N71 from Killarney to Kate Kearney's Cottage, where you can park and begin your trek. Dog-friendly. ///easiest.weep.devoid

130. Ballaghasheen Pass View Point

High atop the windswept peaks of County Kerry, a breathtaking panorama awaits those who venture off the beaten path. Ballaghasheen Pass View Point, a lesser-known gem along the Wild Atlantic Way, rewards visitors with sweeping views of the majestic mountains and verdant valleys that define this captivating region. As you gaze upon the breathtaking landscape, take a moment to appreciate the rich history of the area, which was once traversed by ancient traders following the Butter Road, a historic route used to transport butter to the bustling markets of Cork and beyond.

-> Follow the N70 from Cahersiveen or Waterville, then turn onto the R568 at the sign for Ballaghasheen Pass. Dog-friendly. ///allegation.merged.escalation

129 GAP OF DUNLOE

Where to Eat
in Ring of Kerry

Skelligs Chocolate and Cafe
Located in the picturesque setting of St. Finian's Bay, Skelligs Chocolate and Cafe offers a unique experience. Not only can guests ilge in freshly made chocolates, but they can also witness the chocolate-making process in the open-plan production facility.

-> V23 KV63. Wheelchair Accessible.
///treat.clunk.brokering

The Blind Piper
The Blind Piper is a blend of traditional Irish charm and modern culinary delights. With a diverse menu and a cosy setting, it's a haven for those seeking authentic Irish flavours. The gastropub vibe adds to its allure, making it a popular choice among locals and tourists alike.

-> V93 DD83. Dog-friendly. ///shuttling.contactod.sleepers

O'Carroll's Cove
O'Carroll's Cove offers a mesmerising beachside dining experience. The cove is celebrated for its crystal-clear waters, white sandy beach, and the frequent sightings of dolphins, seals, and other marine life.

-> V23 V2YP. ///panels.submarine.loyalty

The Lobster Bar & Restaurant
With dishes crafted from the freshest catch, The Lobster Bar & Restaurant promises an unforgettable dining experience. The ambiance is relaxed, and the service is top-notch, ensuring patrons leave with cherished memories.

-> V23 CH99. Dog-friendly.
///exposed.subways.barbers

Scarriff Inn Restaurant
Located on the Ring of Kerry, Scarriff Inn Restaurant offers a delightful dining experience with panoramic views. Known for its Irish cuisine, the restaurant is a favorite stop for travellers exploring the scenic route. The ambiance is warm, and the service is commendable, making it a must-visit spot.

-> V23 YX86. ///pollution.verily.alternative

The Oratory
Housed in a beautifully restored old church, The Oratory Gourmet Pizza and Wine Bar offers a unique dining experience in Cahersiveen. The establishment is renowned for its gourmet pizzas, which are crafted with precision and passion. The ambiance is both cosy and divine, with the church's architecture adding a touch of historical charm.

-> V23 FH64. Wheelchari Accessible.
///regenerate.headpiece.smart

Where to Stay
in Ring of Kerry

Hotels
- Park Hotel Kenmare (Wheelchair Accessible)
- Sheen Falls Lodge (Dog-friendly)
- The Killarney Park (Wheelchair Accessible)
- The Europe Hotel & Resort (Wheelchair Accessible)
- The Dunloe Hotel & Gardens (Wheelchair Accessible. Dog-friendly)
- Parknasilla Resort and Spa

Self-Catering Apartments
- Gleesk Pier Cottage (Dog-friendly)
- The Lodge at Friars Glen (Wheelchair Accessible)
- Lakeside House Killarney
- The Grove Cottage (Wheelchair Accessible. Dog-friendly)
- Silver Birch House (Wheelchair Accessible. Dog-friendly)

Campsites

Glenbeg Caravan & Camping
Glenbeg offers a tranquil escape, blending untouched nature with modern conveniences. Ideal for those valuing serenity, it promises a memorable stay amidst Ireland's captivating landscapes.

-> V23 V2YP. Wheelchair accessible. Dog-friendly. ///admissions.lacy.forewarned

Fleming's White Bridge
Set amidst verdant surroundings, Fleming's White Bridge is a haven for campers. Its harmonious mix of nature's beauty and modern comforts ensures a rejuvenating experience for all visitors.

-> V93 K28N. Dog-friendly. ///breezed.gazer.vent

Mannix Point Campsite
Located on the waterfront on the Gulf Stream Coast of The Ring of Kerry, Mannix Point offers a picturesque setting for campers. It has won several national and international awards and is known for its scenic beauty and facilities.

->V23 VN81. Dog-friendly. ///snapping.airfields.supervises

Roadtrip Essentials
in Ring of Kerry

Food Shops
- Lidl, Killarney
- Tesco Superstore, Killarney
- Aldi, Killarney
- Sheehan's Service Station, Kilnabrack
- Aldi, Cahersiveen
- Centra, Waterville
- Aldi, Kenmare
- Lidl, Kenmare

Water Points and CDP
- Centra, Kenmare (Water & CDP)
- Goosey Island MH Park (Water & CDP)
- White Strand Beach (Water Only)
- Ballinskelligs Beach (Water Only)
- Supervalue Car Park, Killarney (Water Only)

Electric Vehicle Charging Points
- ESB Cars: Harbour View Car Park /// sentiments.structured.blacksmith
- Easygo Charge Point: Bantry Bay Port /// unbearably.displaying.readily
- ecars Charge Point: Kenmare Road, Glengariff ///soppy.courtrooms.adjectives
- ESB Charging Station: St Martin's Avenue, CastletownBereHave ///keep.toffee.rudest
- ecars Charge Point: The Square, CastletownBere ///beacon.monkfish.willow
- EasyGo Charging Station: Shelbourne Street, Kenmare ///raven.lots.acquire
- ESB Charging Station: Whyt's Service Statio ///bling.rebuilt.dots

129 GAP OF DUNLOE

SIGHTS

Castles & Historical Sights
- 131. Uragh Stone Circle (Ciorcal Cloch Uragh)
- 137. Ardgroom Stone Circle
- 138. Ballycrovane Ogham Stone
- 146. Dunboy Castle
- 150. Bantry House

Loughs (Laskes)
- 132. Cloonee Lough (Middle)
- 135. Glanmore Lake

Walks
- 133. Derreen Garden (Gairdín Derreen)

Viewpoints
- 134. Caha Pass

Waterfalls
- 136. Healy Pass Waterfall & Tunnel
- 148. The Mare's Tail Waterfall
- 151. Vaughan's Pass

Churches
- 139. Kilcatherine Church

Nature Spots
- 140. The Hag of Beara

Activities
- 141. Allihies Copper Mine Museum

Beaches & Harbours
- 142. Ballydonegan Beach Allihies
- 143. Garinish Beach
- 144. Dursey Sound
- 145. Pulleen Harbor

Towns
- 147. Castletown-Bearhaven
- 149. Glengarriff

Beara and Sheep's Head

Where the sky meets the sea and the emerald hills embrace the horizon, the captivating beauty of the Beara and Sheep's Head region in Ireland reveals itself. This magical corner of County Cork and Kerry invites you to explore its windswept cliffs, verdant hills, and hidden coves.

Embrace the solitude of the Wild Atlantic Way as you meander along narrow roads, framed by a patchwork of mossy stone walls and vibrant wildflowers. Here, in this unspoiled haven, the raw power of nature and the rich tapestry of Irish history intertwine, creating an unforgettable experience that will linger in your heart long after you've left the shores of this captivating region.

In order to reach this region, the closest airport is the Kerry Airport to the east. You can also reach this area easily by public transport, by catching the train to Killarney and then changing to the local bus service. You can also rent a car from here and drive out to the coastline.

Nestled on the southwestern coast of Ireland, the Beara and Sheep's Head region offers visitors a wealth of attractions that showcase the region's diverse natural beauty, cultural heritage, and historical significance.

The Beara Peninsula, stretching across parts of County Cork and Kerry, is home to picturesque villages such as Eyeries and Allihies, ancient stone circles of Ardgroom and Derreenataggart, and the scenic Healy Pass drive. Outdoor enthusiasts can embark on the Beara Way, a 206-kilometre walking trail that traverses the peninsula, or delve into the area's rich past at the Beara Heritage Centre.

Meanwhile, the Sheep's Head Peninsula, situated between Bantry Bay and Dunmanus Bay in West Cork, offers a 175 km walking trail known as the Sheep's Head Way, perfect for exploring the region's stunning landscape and coastal scenery. History lovers can visit the 17th-century Kilcrohane Tower and the Sheep's Head Lighthouse, while charming villages such as Kilcrohane and Ahakista provide local cuisine and traditional Irish music.

With its unspoiled natural beauty, fascinating history, and warm local hospitality, the Beara and Sheep's Head region is a must-visit destination for those seeking an authentic Irish experience. Answer the call of the Wild Atlantic Way and discover the captivating allure of this hidden gem for yourself.

131. Uragh Stone Circle (Ciorcal Cloch Uragh)

Nestled amidst the striking beauty of the Beara Peninsula, a testament to Ireland's ancient past awaits discovery. The Uragh Stone Circle, a Neolithic masterpiece, stands proudly on a small plateau overlooking the serene Cloonee Lough. This enigmatic monument, comprising five megalithic stones, whispers tales of a time long past, drawing visitors into the mysteries of an era shrouded in history. Remarkably, the stones align with the rising sun during the summer solstice, a celestial event that continues to captivate onlookers today. Visiting the Uragh Stone Circle offers a rare opportunity to connect with Ireland's rich heritage while surrounded by the breathtaking beauty of the Beara Peninsula.

->*Follow the R571 to Ardgroom, and turn left onto L1010 by the Lake House B&B. Continue for 3kms, until you reach a small parking area on the left. Follow the well-marked path for a short walk to the stone circle. Dog-friendly.*
///affords.ramming.sentencing

132. Cloonee Lough

Amidst the rugged beauty of the Beara Peninsula, a tranquil oasis of serene waters and lush greenery unfolds before your eyes. Cloonee Lough, one of three interconnected lakes, invites you to bask in the serenity of its picturesque shores. Surrounded by majestic mountains, this idyllic haven is home to a diverse array of flora and fauna, including the rare white-fronted goose, which graces the lough during its winter migration. A visit to Cloonee Lough promises a rejuvenating escape from the hustle and bustle of daily life, as you immerse yourself in the enchanting landscape of Ireland's Wild Atlantic Way.

-> Follow Kenmare to Lauragh and turn left onto the L1010. Continue for 3kms, and you will arrive at the lough. Dog-friendly. ///pleasurably.cheered.mottos

132 CLOONEE LOUGH

133. Derreen Garden (Gairdín Derreen)

A hidden gem on the Beara Peninsula, where vibrant colours and lush greenery intertwine, awaits those who seek solace in nature's embrace. Derreen Garden, a 60-acre haven of subtropical flora, invites you to wander its meandering paths, delighting in the enchanting beauty of its rare plants and ancient trees.

With a unique microclimate, this coastal oasis is home to exotic species from around the world, including the Chilean flame flower that blooms in fiery splenduor. As you explore the garden's tranquil corners, the soothing sound of the nearby sea completes the magical experience that Derreen Garden has to offer.

-> Take the N70 road to Lauragh, and turn left onto the R571. Continue for 1.5kms, and you will find the entrance to the garden on your left. Wheelchair accessible. Dog-friendly. ///blasted.morally.rudder

134. Caha Pass

Winding through the heart of the Beara Peninsula, a breathtaking route unveils the raw beauty and dramatic landscapes of Ireland's Wild Atlantic Way. The Caha Pass, a mountain pass boasting awe-inspiring scenery, guides you through a series of rugged peaks and lush valleys.

As you traverse the pass, be sure to marvel at the engineering feat of the 19th-century tunnels, carved through the solid rock to create a passage between County Cork and County Kerry. The Caha Pass offers a truly unforgettable journey, immersing you in the untamed beauty of Ireland's southwestern coast.

-> Follow the N71 towards Glengarriff. The pass is located along this route, between the two towns, and is 14kms from Kenmare. Wheelchair accessible. Dog-friendly. ///chaos.stimulated.interviewing

134 CAHA PASS

135. Glanmore Lake

Nestled in a verdant valley on the Beara Peninsula, a shimmering expanse of water reflects the majesty of the surrounding mountains. Glanmore Lake, a serene haven of natural beauty, offers a peaceful retreat from the world, where the splendour of the Irish landscape takes centre stage.

The pristine waters of the lake are home to an abundance of brown trout, making it a popular destination for anglers seeking a peaceful fishing experience. As you explore the shores of Glanmore Lake, allow the enchanting beauty of this hidden gem to captivate your senses and rejuvenate your spirit.

-> Follow the R571 road from Kenmare to Lauragh. Approximately 2 kilometers before Lauragh, turn left onto a narrow road signposted for Glanmore Lake. Continue for 3kms, and you will arrive at the lake. Wheelchair accessible. Dog-friendly. ///edited.unifies.refuse

136. Healy Pass Waterfall & Tunnel

Amidst the rugged terrain of the Beara Peninsula, a hidden treasure reveals itself to those who venture off the beaten path. The Healy Pass Waterfall & Tunnel, a captivating blend of natural beauty and human ingenuity, offers a mesmerising spectacle as crystal-clear waters cascade over moss-covered rocks.

The tunnel, carved through the mountainside during the 19th century, stands as a testament to the determination of the Irish people. As you explore this enchanting site, allow the soothing sound of the waterfall to wash away the stresses of daily life and immerse yourself in the timeless allure of Ireland's Wild Atlantic Way.

-> Follow the R574 road from Adrigole to Lauragh. The waterfall is located approximately halfway along the Healy Pass, which is a winding mountain road. Dog-friendly. ///journalists.harmless.scales

137. Cashelkeelty Stone Circle

Step back in time and immerse yourself in the mesmerising beauty of a historical stone circle nestled in the heart of County Kerry. Surrounded by the stunning landscape of the Beara Peninsula, this ancient monument captivates visitors with its enigmatic presence.

The majestic standing stones exude an aura of mystery, transporting you to a time long ago. Legend has it that Cashelkeelty Stone Circle was a sacred meeting place for ancient tribes. Interestingly, this iconic location also offers breathtaking views of the majestic Macgillycuddy's Reeks mountain range.

-> To reach the site, follow N70 road towards Sneem. You will find a small car park on the left after Lauragh. Dog-friendly. ///mentioning.tend.vest

138. Ballycrovane Ogham Stone

In the rugged landscape of Ireland's Beara Peninsula stands a towering testament to the region's ancient past. The Ballycrovane Ogham Stone, an impressive monolith reaching over 5 metres in height, is the tallest of its kind in Ireland. Bearing inscriptions in the ancient Ogham script, this enigmatic stone whispers tales of a time long ago, when Celtic tribes inhabited the land. As you stand in the presence of this awe-inspiring monument, allow yourself to be transported to a bygone era, connecting with the rich heritage and enduring spirit of Ireland's ancestors.

-> Follow the R572 to Kilcatherine. Approximately 3kms after Kilcatherine, turn left onto a narrow road signposted for the Ogham Stone. Continue for 1.5kms and the site is on the left. Dog-friendly. ///inhale.necessary.microwave

139. Kilcatherine Church

Perched on a windswept hill overlooking the rugged Beara Peninsula, the hauntingly beautiful ruins of Kilcatherine Church beckon to those seeking solace and serenity. Steeped in history, this sacred site dates back to the 7th century and is dedicated to Saint Caitighearn, a revered figure in Irish folklore.

As you wander through the remnants of this ancient place of worship, take a moment to appreciate the intricately carved stone cross, a testament to the skill and devotion of the craftsmen who created it. Amidst the whispers of the past, allow the breathtaking beauty of Kilcatherine Church to inspire your soul and ignite your imagination.

-> Upon entering Kilcatherine, turn left onto a narrow road signposted for the church. Continue for 1km, and you will find the site on your left. ///surged.cased.declining

139 KILCATHERINE CHURCH

136 HEALY PASS WATERFALL & TUNNEL

140. The Hag of Beara

Enshrouded in myth and legend, a mysterious figure stands sentinel over the wild and windswept Beara Peninsula. The Hag of Beara, a striking rock formation, is said to be the petrified remains of an ancient wise woman, a powerful figure in Irish folklore.

As you gaze upon this enigmatic guardian, allow the magic of the landscape to envelop you, and feel the echoes of ancient tales reverberate through the ages. Embrace the enchanting allure of this storied land, and let the spirit of the Hag of Beara weave its spell upon your heart.

-> *2 kilometres before Allihies, turn left onto a narrow road signposted for the Hag of Beara. Continue for 1km, and you will find the site on your left. ///fond.shoppers.soothingly*

141. Allihies Copper Mine Museum

Nestled in the picturesque village of Allihies, a fascinating window into the past awaits to transport you to the days of Ireland's industrial heritage. The Allihies Copper Mine Museum, housed in a beautifully restored Methodist church, offers a captivating glimpse into the lives of the miners who once toiled in the depths of the earth. Discover the rich history of the copper mining industry, which thrived in the area during the 19th century, and marvel at the ingenuity and resilience of the people who shaped this rugged landscape.

-> *Follow the R572 from Castletownbere to Allihies. Upon entering the village, you will find the museum on your left. Wheelchair accessible. Dog-friendly. ///ladder.marvel.sorbets*

140 THE HAG OF BEARA

142. Ballydonegan Beach

A hidden gem awaits on the rugged Beara Peninsula, where the wild Atlantic waves meet the pristine sands of Ballydonegan Beach in Allihies. This idyllic haven, unique for its copper-infused sands, offers a serene escape from the hustle and bustle of everyday life. As you stroll along the shoreline, breathe in the invigorating sea air, and let the soothing sound of the waves wash away your cares. Embrace the enchanting beauty of Ballydonegan Beach, and allow the magic of Ireland's Wild Atlantic Way to captivate your heart and soul.

-> Follow the R572 from Castletownbere to Allihies. Upon entering the village, follow the signs for the beach, which is located just a short distance from the village centre. Dog-friendly. ///banish.moderating.summers

143. Garinish Beach

Tucked away on the breathtaking Beara Peninsula lies a secluded paradise, where the azure waters of the Atlantic Ocean embrace the golden sands of Garinish Beach. This tranquil oasis, renowned for its crystal-clear water and stunning natural beauty, invites you to lose yourself in the serenity of Ireland's Wild Atlantic Way. As you explore this enchanting haven, take a moment to appreciate the vibrant marine life that thrives in the surrounding waters, a testament to the pristine nature of this coastal gem.

-> Follow the R572 from Castletownbere to Adrigole. Upon entering Adrigole, turn left onto the R575 road, and continue for 4kms. Turn right onto a narrow road signposted for Garinish Beach, and follow it to the beach. Dog-friendly. ///toys.sunken.bookings

143 GARINISH BEACH

144. Dursey Sound

At the southwestern tip of the Beara Peninsula, a dramatic meeting of land and sea unfolds in a spectacular display of nature's power. Dursey Sound, a narrow channel separating Dursey Island from the mainland, boasts a breathtaking vista of rugged cliffs, crashing waves, and a multitude of seabirds soaring overhead.

As you marvel at the incredible beauty of this remote haven, keep an eye out for the unique cable car that ferries visitors across the Sound, the only one of its kind in Ireland.

-> *Follow the R572 to Allihies. Continue past Allihies, and follow the signs for Dursey Island. The cable car station is located approximately 10kms from Allihies. Wheelchair accessible. Dog-friendly. ///preheated.carnivore.reflective*

145. Pulleen Harbour

Nestled along the rugged Beara Peninsula, a serene haven of natural beauty and tranquility awaits discovery. Pulleen Harbour, a picturesque cove sheltered by imposing cliffs, offers a peaceful retreat from the world's hustle and bustle.

As you stand at the water's edge, feel the gentle caress of the sea breeze and listen to the soothing lullaby of the waves. Gaze upon the vibrant marine life that thrives in the crystal-clear waters, a testament to the pristine nature of this coastal gem.

-> *Follow the R572 towards Allihies. 7kms from Castletownbere, turn left onto a narrow road signposted for Pulleen Harbour, and follow it to the cove. Wheelchair accessible. Dog-friendly. ///scheduled.irrigation.hurdle*

144 DURSEY SOUND

146. Dunboy Castle

Steeped in history and shrouded in mystery, the ruins of a once-magnificent fortress stand sentinel over the rugged Beara Peninsula. Dunboy Castle, a 15th-century stronghold of the O'Sullivan Bere clan, whispers tales of rebellion, conquest, and the indomitable spirit of the Irish people. As you explore the crumbling remnants of this storied edifice, imagine the fierce battles that raged within its walls, and let the echoes of the past envelop you in their timeless embrace.

Amidst the haunting beauty of the castle's ruins, discover the poignant memorial to the Flight of the Earls, a pivotal event in Irish history that marked the end of Gaelic rule.

-> Follow the R572 road from Castletownbere towards Allihies. Turn right onto the R575 road, and continue for approximately 2kms. Turn left onto a narrow road signposted for Dunboy Castle, and follow it to the castle ruins. Dog-friendly. ///paperbacks.recycling.absorb

147. Castletown-Bearhaven

A picturesque haven nestled along the Wild Atlantic Way, Castletown-Bearhaven beckons visitors with its charming streets, vibrant shops, and warm hospitality. This bustling fishing port, the largest town on the Beara Peninsula, boasts a rich seafaring heritage that is proudly displayed in its colourful boats, lively waterfront, and historic landmarks. As you wander through the town, take a moment to appreciate the stunning views of Bantry Bay and the distant Caha Mountains, a breathtaking backdrop that perfectly complements the town's lively atmosphere.

-> Follow the R572 road from Glengarriff or Kenmare. The town is well-signed and easily accessible from the main road. Wheelchair accessible. Dog-friendly. ///brunch.competency.scrubbing

146 DUNBOY CASTLE

148. Hungry Hill

Rising majestically in the Beara Peninsula, a grand summit beckons adventurous souls to conquer its rugged slopes. This lofty peak, shrouded in mysticism and folklore, offers an exhilarating journey for hikers and nature enthusiasts alike. As you ascend, your every step unveils panoramic vistas that leave you breathless, from the sweeping valleys to the glistening lakes below. An interesting fact about this area is that Hungry Hill derives its name from a local legend of a famine-stricken family who faced great hardship while dwelling there.

-> Parking available at entrance to Park Road from the R572. Path follows the Park Road for 1km before turning up the hill. Only suitable for experienced hillwalkers or groups accompanied by experienced hillwalker. Hiking map is required with compass. ///domes.perspectives.boundary

149. Glengarriff

Enveloped in lush greenery and surrounded by the enchanting Caha Mountains, a charming village beckons with its warm Irish hospitality and breathtaking natural beauty. Glengarriff, meaning "Rugged Glen" in Irish, serves as a gateway to the Beara Peninsula and offers visitors a delightful array of attractions, such as the famous Garnish Island and its exquisite Italian gardens.

Did you know that Glengarriff boasts one of the oldest nature reserves in Ireland, home to ancient oak forests and a thriving population of native red squirrels?

-> Follow the N71 road from Kenmare or Bantry. The village is well-signposted and easily accessible from the main road. Wheelchair accessible. Dog-friendly. ///dumped.gels.pantomime

150. Bantry House

A majestic testament to Ireland's rich history and architectural prowess, an elegant estate stands proudly overlooking the shimmering waters of Bantry Bay. Bantry House, once the ancestral home of the Earls of Bantry, enchants visitors with its exquisite gardens, opulent interiors, and fascinating collection of art and artifacts. This stunning 18th-century mansion also played a crucial role in thwarting a French invasion during the 1796 Battle of Bantry Bay.

-> Follow the N71 road into Bantry town. The estate is well-signposted and easily accessible from the main road. There is ample parking available on-site. Wheelchair accessible on the ground floor and gardens. Dog-friendly in the gardens. ///sender.hobbling.bushes

151. Vaughan's Pass

Winding through the rugged beauty of the Caha Mountains, a scenic mountain pass captivates the hearts of all who traverse its serpentine path. Vaughan's Pass offers breathtaking panoramas of the Beara Peninsula and Bantry Bay, rewarding adventurous travellers with unforgettable views. Interestingly, this incredible route was originally constructed during the Great Famine as a public works project to provide employment for the local population.

-> Follow the R572 towards Adrigole. 4kms from Lauragh, turn onto the R574 road, which will take you through the pass. The road is narrow but well-maintained, and suitable for most vehicles. Wheelchair accessible. Dog-friendly. ///cheeky.sanity.forces

Where to Eat
in Beara and Sheep's Head

No. 35
A culinary gem in Kenmare, No. 35 offers a delightful array of dishes that showcase the richness of local produce. The ambiance is intimate, making it perfect for romantic dinners or special occasions.

-> V93 Y038. ///spruce.therapies.experimental

Murphy's Restaurant
Celebrated for its diverse Irish and international dishes, the restaurant particularly shines with its seafood offerings. The ambiance, characterised by warm lighting and tasteful decor, complements the dining experience, making every meal feel special.

-> V93 EFP1. ///furthering.testified.tagline

Breen's Lobster Bar & Restaurant
Breen's, in the heart of Castletownbere, is a seafood lover's paradise. With fresh catches daily, it offers an authentic taste of the ocean. The cosy ambiance and impeccable service make every meal a memorable culinary journey.

-> P75T862. Wheelchair Accessible. ///strikeout.ailing.wipers

Helen's Bar
A magical spot offering a blend of Irish cuisine, especially seafood. Known for its enchanting views and top-notch service, it's a must-visit for both the ambiance and the culinary delights.

-> V93 NF70. ///endearing.cartoonist.clockwork

Sugarloaf Cafe
A cosy cafe in Glengarriff, Sugarloaf offers a range of delectable treats and beverages. With its laid-back atmosphere and friendly staff, it's the ideal spot for a leisurely afternoon or a quick snack.

-> P75 AK71. Wheelchair Accessible. ///crushing.project.slurs

Casey's Bar and Restaurant
A renowned establishment in Glengarriff, Casey's Bar and Restaurant promises a gastronomic journey. With its diverse menu and rustic charm, it's a favourite among locals and tourists alike.

-> V93 T289. ///trickle.patches.awaits

148 HUNGRY HILL

Where to Stay
in Beara and Sheep's Head

Hotels
- Casey's Hotel, Glengarriff
- Eccles Hotel and Spa (Wheelchair accessible)
- Berehaven Pods
- Rugged Glen Accommodation
- Beara Coast Hotel
- Park Hotel Kenmare (Wheelchair accessible)

Self-Catering Apartments
- Berehaven Lodge (Wheelchair accessible. Dog-friendly)
- Allihies Holiday Homes (Wheelchair accessible. Dog-friendly)
- Beara Holiday Homes
- Tir na Hilan Self Catering
- Seal Cottage (Wheelchair Accessible. Dog-friendly)

Campsites

Beara Camping
Beara Camping offers a serene environment for campers, nestled amidst the natural beauty of the Beara Peninsula. It's an ideal spot for those looking to explore the surrounding areas of Kenmare and Kerry.

-> V93 YP29. ///underwear.trawlers.incorrect

Hungry Hill Lodge & Campsite
Hungry Hill Lodge and Campsite is a family-friendly holiday park that combines the rustic charm of camping with the luxury of glamping. Set in the heart of the Beara Peninsula, it promises an unforgettable outdoor experience.

-> P75 CY62. Dog-friendly. ///laminated.overfed.fulfilling

Eyeries MotorHome Park
Eyeries MotorHome Park provides campers with a tranquil setting on the Beara Peninsula. With its strategic location, it's a great starting point for exploring the region's natural wonders and attractions.

-> P75 WY02. ///screamed.mercenary.decorate

138 BALLYCROVANE OGHAM STONE

Roadtrip Essentials
in Beara and Sheep's Head

Food Shops
- Spar, Castletownbere
- SuperValu, Castletownbere
- Spar, Glengariff
- Lidl, Bantry
- SuperValu, Bantry

Water Points and CDP
- Coulagh Bay Harbour (Water Only)
- Beara Holiday Homes, Garinish (Water & CDP)
- Castletownbere Harbour (Water Only)
- Adrigole Harbour (Water Only)
- Glengariff Harbour (Water Only)

Electric Vehicle Charging Points
- "ESB Cars: Harbour View Car Park /// sentiments.structured.blacksmith
- Easygo Charge Point: Bantry Bay Port /// unbearably.displaying.readily
- ecars Charge Point: Kenmare Road, Glengariff ///soppy.courtrooms.adjectives
- ESB Charging Station: St Martin's Avenue, CastletownBereHave ///keep.toffee.rudest
- ecars Charge Point: The Square, CastletownBere ///beacon.monkfish.willow
- EasyGo Charging Station: Shelbourne Street, Kenmare ///raven.lots.acquire
- ESB Charging Station: Whyt's Service Station ///bling.rebuilt.dots"

135 GLANMORE LAKE

136 HEALY PASS WATERFALL & TUNNEL

SIGHTS

Castles & Historical Sights
- 152. Altar Wedge Tomb
- 158. Aughadown Graveyard
- 161. Cnoc Droma - Knockdrum Stone Fort
- 162. Drombeg Stone Circle
- 165. Timoleague Friary
- 168. Charles Fort
- 170. Coppingers Court

Beaches & Harbours
- 153. Barleycove
- 163. Long Strand
- 164. Inchydoney Beach

Viewpoints
- 154. Mizen Head
- 159. Baltimore Beacon
- 167. Old Head of Kinsale

Towns
- 155. Crookhaven
- 166. Courtmacsherry
- 169. Cobh
- 171. Cork

Mountains
- 156. Mount Gabriel

Island
- 157. Cape Clear
- 160. Sherkin Island

West Cork

In the heart of Ireland's enchanting southwest, a land of untamed beauty and timeless charm beckons the wanderer's soul. West Cork, a place where the earth and sea conspire to paint a landscape of breathtaking grandeur, hints at the ancient secrets of its rugged coastlines and verdant hills.

Here, the Wild Atlantic Way gives promise of a journey filled with adventure and discovery, its winding roads guiding you through a realm of wonder and serenity. Extending from Ballydehob to Kinsale, this coastal stretch presents an inviting chance for visitors to embrace a leisurely pace and immerse themselves in the tranquil charm of the most sheltered section along the extensive Wild Atlantic Way.

In order to reach this region, the closest airport is Cork Airport. You can also reach this area easily by public transport, by catching the train to Cork and then changing to the local bus service. You can also rent a car from here and drive out to the coastline.

171 CORK

162 DROMBEG STONE CIRCLE

Nestled along Ireland's southwestern coastline, West Cork is a treasure trove of natural beauty, rich history, and vibrant culture. Renowned for its picturesque towns and villages, such as Kinsale, Clonakilty, and Skibbereen, this captivating region offers a diverse array of attractions and activities for visitors to explore.

From the breathtaking Mizen Head, Ireland's most south westerly point, to the tranquil Lough Hyne, the country's first marine nature reserve, West Cork's diverse landscape provides ample opportunities for outdoor pursuits, including hiking, cycling, and water sports. History enthusiasts will delight in the region's wealth of ancient sites and monuments, such as Drombeg Stone Circle, while food lovers can indulge in West Cork's thriving culinary scene, which boasts a plethora of artisan producers, farmers' markets, and award-winning restaurants.

With its unique blend of stunning scenery, rich heritage, and warm hospitality, West Cork is a destination that promises an unforgettable experience for all who journey to its enchanting shores.

152. Altar Wedge Tomb

Steeped in the shadows of time, an ancient burial site stands sentinel over the rugged landscape of West Cork. The Altar Wedge Tomb, dating back to the Bronze Age, offers a glimpse into the distant past, when Ireland's ancestors honoured their departed with these enigmatic stone structures. Intriguingly, the tomb derives its name from the mistaken belief that it was an altar used by Catholic priests during the Penal Laws era, when the practice of Catholicism was forbidden.

-> *Follow the R592 towards Toormore. Turn left at the signpost for Altar Church, and continue for 1km until you reach a small parking area. From there, a short walk along a gravel path leads to the tomb. Dog-friendly.*
///poodles.parklands.affiliation

153. Barleycove

Nestled along the breathtaking Mizen Peninsula, a stunning coastal haven entices visitors with its sweeping dunes and pristine shores. Barleycove, a Blue Flag beach, is renowned for its exceptional beauty and unspoiled surroundings. Even driving along the road you can admire the beauty of Barleycove Beach. Interestingly, the area's impressive sand dunes were formed by a tidal wave following the 1755 Lisbon earthquake, leaving behind a unique and captivating landscape.

-> *Take the R591 towards Crookhaven. After 4kms, turn left onto a minor road signposted for Barleycove Beach. Continue for about 1.5kms to the beach's parking area. Dog-friendly. ///bigger.bending.irritably*

153 BARLEYCOVE

154. Mizen Head

At the edge of the world, where the land meets the sea, a breathtaking spectacle of nature's grandeur unfolds. Ireland's most southwesterly point, Mizen Head, captivates the soul with its dramatic cliffs and panoramic ocean views, where the mighty waves of the Atlantic crash against the rugged coastline.

This stunning destination is home to the iconic Mizen Head Signal Station, which has guided mariners for over a century. Remarkably, the station's suspension bridge, once the longest in Europe, spans the churning waters below, connecting the mainland to the rocky outcrop where the signal station stands.

-> Take the R591 towards Crookhaven, and follow the signs for Mizen Head. The journey is 8kms from Goleen. Wheelchair accessible. Dog-friendly. ///package.utopia.shirk

155. Crookhaven

A charming coastal village steeped in maritime history beckons visitors to explore its picturesque harbour and welcoming atmosphere. Crookhaven, nestled along the rugged Mizen Peninsula, once served as the last port of call for sailing ships bound for America, providing safe haven and provisions before their arduous journey across the Atlantic.

Today, this enchanting village delights with its colourful cottages, lively pubs, and breathtaking sea views, making it an ideal destination for a leisurely stroll or a relaxing meal by the water's edge.

-> Follow the R591 road from Goleen for 5kms. Wheelchair accessible. Dog-friendly. ///restless.marry.consumed

154 MIZEN HEAD

154 MIZEN HEAD

156. Mount Gabriel

Rising majestically above the idyllic coastal landscape, a sentinel of nature's beauty and ancient history casts its watchful gaze across West Cork. Mount Gabriel, the highest peak in the region, offers breathtaking panoramic views of the Mizen Peninsula and the surrounding countryside.

Intriguingly, the mountain's slopes are home to two Bronze Age copper mines, bearing witness to the region's rich archaeological heritage and providing a fascinating glimpse into the lives of Ireland's early inhabitants.

-> Follow the R591 road from Schull towards Goleen. 3kms outside Schull, turn left onto a minor road signposted for Mount Gabriel. Continue for about 2kms, following the signs to the mountain's summit. Dog-friendly.
///toothpicks.regularity.markets

157. Cape Clear

A remote island paradise steeped in ancient lore and breathtaking beauty awaits discovery off the coast of West Cork. Cape Clear, Ireland's southernmost inhabited island, offers a tranquil retreat from the bustle of modern life, with its rugged cliffs, pristine beaches, and abundant wildlife. This part of West Cork is facinatingly unique due to the large number of artifacts, such as the Cape Clear Stone, that are remnants of the Boyne Valley Civillisation. This group of people were thought to mainly dwell in the north of Ireland and these relics are not normally found in Southern Ireland, much less on an island off the coast of West Cork.

-> Take a ferry from Baltimore or Schull, with regular services available during the summer months and a limited schedule during the off-season. Dog-friendly.
///pings.blizzards.blazers

158. Aughadown Graveyard

Steeped in history and shrouded in an air of tranquility, a sacred resting place lies nestled amidst the rolling hills of West Cork. Aughadown Graveyard, an ancient burial ground, bears witness to the passage of time and the lives of those who have come before us. Amongst the weathered headstones and Celtic crosses, the final resting place of Tadhg Ó Donnabháin, a famed Irish poet from the 18th century, can be found, connecting the present with the rich literary heritage of the past.

-> *Follow the N71 road from Skibbereen towards Bantry. 7kms outside Skibbereen, turn left onto the R594 road towards Church Cross. Continue for 4kms, then turn right onto a minor road, following the signs to the graveyard's location. ///serve.cabbages.traceable*

159. Baltimore Beacon

Perched atop a windswept cliff, a sentinel of stone stands watch over the wild Atlantic waves, guiding mariners through the treacherous waters off Ireland's southern coast. The Baltimore Beacon, affectionately known as 'Lot's Wife,' has been a steadfast guardian of seafarers since its construction in 1849, its striking white pillar a comforting sight amidst the ever-changing seascape. This iconic landmark offers visitors breathtaking panoramic views and a tangible connection to the region's maritime heritage.

-> *Upon entering Baltimore village, turn right onto the R595 road towards the harbour. Continue for about 1km, then turn left at the signpost for the Beacon. Follow the narrow road uphill until you reach the parking area, from which a short walk will lead you to the Beacon itself. Dog-friendly. ///unhurried.wilt.toil*

157 CAPE CLEAR

160. Sherkin Island

A haven of tranquility and unspoiled beauty beckons just a stone's throw from the bustling harbour of Baltimore. Sherkin Island, the 'Island of the Poets,' captivates the hearts of visitors with its pristine beaches, vibrant artistic community, and rich historical tapestry.

The island's unique charm is further enhanced by the Sherkin Friary, a 15th-century Franciscan monastery that stands as a testament to the region's ecclesiastical heritage. With over 100 species of birds recorded, Sherkin Island is also a birdwatcher's paradise, offering a glimpse into the diverse avian life that calls this enchanting isle home.

-> *Take a ferry from Baltimore, with regular services available throughout the year. Dog-friendly.*
///chipped.hurls.tempted

161. Cnoc Droma - Knockdrum Stone Fort

Whispers of a bygone era permeate the air as ancient stone walls reveal a glimpse into Ireland's distant past. Cnoc Droma, or Knockdrum Stone Fort, stands as a testament to the early Celtic settlers who once inhabited this land over a thousand years ago. This well-preserved hilltop enclosure offers not only a fascinating insight into the region's history but also boasts breathtaking panoramic views of the surrounding countryside and coastline, including the iconic Fastnet Rock Lighthouse.

-> *Follow the N71 towards Castletownshend. 5kms outside Skibbereen, turn left onto the R596 road towards Castletownshend. Continue for about 3kms, then turn right onto a minor road, following the signs to Knockdrum Stone Fort. Dog-friendly.*///valve.journalists.bristles

161 CNOC DROMA - KNOCKDRUM STONE FORT

162. Drombeg Stone Circle

Steeped in mystery and ancient lore, a captivating monument whispers tales of a time long past. Drombeg Stone Circle, also known as the Druid's Altar, stands as a testament to Ireland's rich prehistoric heritage.

This Bronze Age ceremonial site, comprising 17 standing stones, offers a fascinating glimpse into the lives of those who once walked this land. With its precise alignment to the winter solstice sunset, the stone circle showcases the remarkable astronomical knowledge of its builders, leaving visitors in awe of the skill and ingenuity of our ancestors.

-> Follow the N71 towards Glandore. 5kms outside Glandore, turn right onto a minor road, following the signs to Drombeg Stone Circle. Continue for about 2kms until you reach the site. Dog-friendly. ///peering.dippy.pots

163. Long Strand

Where the wild Atlantic waves meet a pristine stretch of coastline, a haven of tranquility and natural beauty unfolds. Long Strand, a magnificent 2-kilometre expanse of sandy shore in West Cork, enchants visitors with its breathtaking scenery and invigorating sea air.

Flanked by majestic sand dunes, home to a diverse array of flora and fauna, this captivating destination offers a serene escape for beachcombers and nature enthusiasts alike. With its strong currents and powerful waves, Long Strand attracts surfers seeking an adrenaline-fueled adventure amidst the ever-changing tides.

-> Upon entering Rosscarbery, turn right onto the R597 and continue for approximately 7kms. Then, turn right onto a minor road, following the signs to Long Strand. Continue for about 2kms until you reach the beach. Dog-friendly. ///methodical.wirelessly.spaceship

164. Inchydoney Beach

A breathtaking panorama of golden sands and azure waves greets visitors as they embark on a journey to a coastal paradise. Inchydoney Beach, a stunning stretch of shoreline in West Cork, has been consistently voted as one of Ireland's most beautiful beaches.

Its crystal-clear waters and gentle slopes make it an ideal destination for families and those who enjoy cold water swimming. With the Gulf Stream's warming influence, the area boasts a unique microclimate that nurtures a diverse range of marine life, offering a fascinating underwater world for snorkelers and divers to explore.

-> Follow the N71 towards Clonakilty. Upon entering Clonakilty, turn left onto the R599 and continue for approximately 4kms. Then, turn right onto a minor road, following the signs to Inchydoney Beach. Wheelchair accessible. Dog-friendly. ///chuckling.attracted.miniskirt

165. Timoleague Friary

Steeped in history and shrouded in mystery, the ancient ruins of a once-thriving monastic community invite the curious to discover. Timoleague Friary, a 13th-century Franciscan abbey nestled along the banks of the picturesque Argideen River, stands as a testament to the passage of time and the resilience of faith.

Its crumbling walls and intricate stone carvings whisper tales of a bygone era, inviting visitors to step back in time and immerse themselves in the rich heritage of this sacred site. The friary's enchanting setting offers a unique blend of natural beauty and spiritual solace, leaving a lasting impression on all who wander its hallowed grounds.

-> Follow the N71 towards Clonakilty. Turn left onto the R599 road and continue for 2kms. Then, turn right onto a minor road, following the signs to Dunworley Beach. Dog-friendly. ///howled.duped.outlines

166. Courtmacsherry

A charming seaside village awaits, where time seems to slow down and the worries of the world fade away. Courtmacsherry, is a true gem of West Cork, enchanting visitors with its quaint streets, colourful houses, and breathtaking coastal views. This idyllic, picturesque village is steeped in maritime history, as it is home to one of the oldest lifeboat stations in Ireland, established in 1825.

Stroll along the peaceful shoreline, bask in the warmth of the sun, and enjoy the tranquility of Courtmacsherry.

-> Upon entering Clonakilty, turn left onto the R599 road and continue for 2kms. Then, turn right onto the R600 road and continue for about 14kms until you reach Courtmacsherry village. Wheelchair accessible. Dog-friendly. ///ogles.call.spenders

165 TIMOLEAGUE FRIARY

167. Old Head of Kinsale

Majestic cliffs rise from the sea, standing sentinel over a breathtaking landscape where land meets water in a dramatic display of nature's splendour. The Old Head of Kinsale, a striking promontory jutting out into the Atlantic Ocean, offers magical views and a rich history.

This iconic landmark played a pivotal role during the sinking of the Lusitania in 1915, as it served as the closest point of land to the tragic event. As visitors traverse the rugged terrain, they are enveloped by the raw beauty and poignant echoes of the past that resonate throughout this unforgettable locale.

-> Upon entering Clonakilty, turn left onto the R600 road and continue for 35kms until you reach Kinsale. From Kinsale, follow the R604 road for about 10kms until you reach the Old Head of Kinsale. Dog-friendly.///snows.rattler.drumming

168. Charles Fort

A sentinel of the past stands proudly on the edge of the sea, its imposing walls whispering tales of battles and bravery. Charles Fort, a 17th-century star-shaped fortress, has guarded the picturesque harbour of Kinsale for centuries. This architectural marvel, steeped in history, offers visitors a unique glimpse into Ireland's military past.

The fort's strategic location played a crucial role during the Williamite War in 1690, a testament to its enduring significance. As you explore the vast grounds and well-preserved ramparts, you'll be transported back in time, captivated by the fort's timeless allure and breathtaking views.

-> From Kinsale, follow the R600 for about 3kms until you reach Charles Fort. Partially wheelchair accessible. Dog-friendly. ///kegs.heading.wiping

169. Cobh

Steeped in maritime history and adorned with brightly colored houses, a picturesque coastal town beckons visitors to explore its rich heritage and breathtaking scenery. Cobh, the last port of call for the ill-fated Titanic, offers a poignant journey into the past, with its Titanic Experience museum and the captivating stories of Irish emigration at the Cobh Heritage Centre.

Stroll along the charming waterfront promenade, or marvel at the architectural grandeur of St. Colman's Cathedral, which boasts one of the largest carillons in Europe. As you immerse yourself in the vibrant culture and captivating tales of this enchanting town, you'll be captivated by the warm embrace of Irish hospitality.

-> From Kinsale, follow the R600 for about 20kms until you reach Carrigaline. From Carrigaline, take the R612 for about 6kms until you reach Crosshaven. Wheelchair accessible. Dog-friendly. ///culminates.also.clinically

170. Coppingers Court

Whispers of a bygone era echo through the ruins of a once-grand estate, inviting visitors to explore the mysteries of its past. Coppingers Court, a 17th-century fortified manor house, stands as a testament to the opulence and ambition of its original owner, Sir Walter Coppinger.

This intriguing historical site, now a hauntingly beautiful shell of its former glory, offers a fascinating glimpse into Ireland's architectural heritage. As you wander among the ivy-clad walls and crumbling archways, you'll be captivated by the stories and legends that surround this enigmatic monument to a vanished age.

-> From Crosshaven, continue on the R612 road for about 7kms, then turn left onto an unnamed road and drive for 1.5kms to reach Coppingers Court. Care must be taken inside as it is a ruin. ///wirelessly.dine.medallion

171. Cork

A vibrant city brimming with history, culture, and a lively spirit, Ireland's second-largest metropolis captivates visitors with its unique charm. Known as the "Rebel City" due to its role in the Irish War of Independence, Cork boasts a rich variety of historical landmarks, including the iconic St. Fin Barre's Cathedral and the atmospheric English Market, which has been serving local fare since 1788. As you wander through the bustling streets and quaint alleyways, you'll be enchanted by the city's warmth and energy, as well as the friendly locals who are always eager to share a story or a smile.

-> Follow the N71 road towards Clonakilty for approximately 85kms. Wheelchair-accessible. Dog-friendly. ///giving.rock.supper

171 CORK

Where to Eat
in West Cork

The Fish Kitchen
Situated in the heart of Bantry, The Fish Kitchen is a seafood lover's paradise. Renowned for its daily fresh catches, this restaurant prides itself on serving the finest seafood dishes. With its minimalist yet inviting setting, diners are treated to an authentic taste of the sea in a relaxed atmosphere.

-> PL29 3RH. Wheelchair Accessible. Dog-friendly. ///swatted.sorry.sprang

Casey's of Baltimore
Overlooking the serene waters of Baltimore, Casey's offers a delightful blend of traditional Irish flavours and modern culinary techniques. The restaurant's cosy ambiance, complemented by panoramic views, has made it a cherished spot for both locals and tourists seeking a memorable dining experience.

-> P81 YW66. Wheelchair Accessible. ///divided.wardrobes.embodying

Scannells Bar
Set in the bustling town of Clonakilty, Scannells Bar is more than just a dining spot. It's a fusion of traditional pub vibes with contemporary dining. Known for its broad menu, live music sessions, and warm hospitality, it's a place where food, music, and culture intertwine.

-> T85 T938. Wheelchair Accessible. Dog-friendly. ///tweeting.uncle.scrabbling

The Glandore Inn
Perched on the edge of Glandore Harbour, The Glandore Inn is a gem of West Cork. With its breathtaking views of the coast, diners can savour a menu rich in local produce. The inn's warm and welcoming atmosphere makes it a top choice for those seeking a tranquil dining setting.

-> P81 WE16. Dog-friendly. ///letter.playlists.coursework

The Bulman Bar & Restaurant
Located in the historic town of Kinsale, The Bulman Bar & Restaurant is a fusion of history, culinary excellence, and scenic beauty. Specialising in seafood dishes, its waterside location provides diners with both gastronomic delights and mesmerising views of the sea.

-> P17 TH76. Dog-friendly. ///password.invited.immovable

Greenes Restaurant
Tucked away in Cork City, Greenes Restaurant stands out with its innovative European cuisine. With a focus on locally-sourced ingredients and modern culinary techniques, the restaurant offers a unique dining experience. The contemporary decor, paired with a cascading waterfall, adds to its urban charm and elegance.

-> T23 F6EK. Wheelchair Accessible. ///giant.match.stones

164 INCHYDONEY BEACH

Where to Stay
in West Cork

Hotels
- Schull Harbour Hotel & Leisure Centre (Wheelchair Accessible. Dog-friendly)
- Celtic Ross Hotel (Wheelchair Accessible)
- The Barleycove Beach Hotel
- The Waterfront Hotel (Dog-friendly)
- Actons Hotel Kinsale (Wheelchair Accessible)
- The Imperial Hotel & Spa (Wheelchair Accessible. Dog-friendly)

Self-Catering Apartments
- Rock Cottage Country House
- Cute Coastal Village Retreat, Castletownshend
- Corr an Droma
- Dunowen House, Clonakilty
- 1 Closheen Lane, Ross Carbery (Dog-friendly)

Campsites

Barleycove Holiday Park
A picturesque coastal retreat located near Mizen Head, Barleycove Holiday Park offers stunning beach views, modern amenities, and a serene environment, making it a top choice for families and nature enthusiasts.
-> P81 X074. ///bathrobes.measuring.choice

The Hideaway Camping & Caravan Park
Nestled in Skibbereen, The Hideaway provides a tranquil setting with top-notch facilities. Its proximity to the coast and the town's attractions makes it a favoured spot for both seasoned campers and first-timers.
->Dog-friendly. ///defining.language.fearlessly

Sextons Caravan & Camping
Situated in Timoleague, Sextons Caravan & Camping boasts scenic landscapes and a range of amenities. Its coastal location and welcoming atmosphere ensure a memorable camping experience for visitors of all ages.
-> P72 WY61. Wheelchair Accessible. Dog-friendly. ///incoherent.graduating.krill

Roadtrip Essentials
in West Cork

Food Shops
- Lidl, Batry
- Ryan's Village Grocer, Durrus
- Centra, Schull
- Lidl, Skibbereen
- Aldi, Skibbereen
- Lodis, Rosscarberry
- Lidl, Clonakilty
- Aldi, Clonakilty
- Centra, Timoleague
- Lidl, Kinsale
- Spar, Kinsale

Water Points and CDP
- Westlodge Hotel (Water & CDP)
- Bantry Pier (Water & CDP)
- Schull Harbour (Water Only)
- Baltimore Pier (Water Only)
- Tragumna Beach (Water Only)
- Timoleague Public Toilets (Water Only)
- Kinsale Public Toilets (Water Only)
- Midleton Town Centre (Water & CDP)

Electric Vehicle Charging Points
- eCars Charge Point: The Square, CastletownBere ///beacon.monkfish.willow
- Easygo Charge Point: Bantry Bay Port ///unbearably.displaying.readily
- ecars Charge Point: Deasy's Car Park, Clonakilty ///showering.thirst.deluxe
- EasyGo Charging Station: Scally's SuperValu, Clonakilty ///emigrate.crooked.transforming
- Tesla Destination Charger: The Clonakilty Hotel ///inferences.cons.regulate
- ESB Charging Point: Tesco Superstore, Mallow ///jiving.transitions.ornaments
- ePower Charging Station: Cork Airpor ///waddle.sting.birds
- Tesla Supercharger: Mahon Point Shopping Centre ///dividers.preparing.chopped
- ESB Charging Station: Circle K Service Station, Frankfield ///frog.rainy.couple
- Q-Park Charge Point: City Hall Car Park, Ballintemple ///pipe.acute.bills
- ChargePoint Charging Station: Cork County Hall ///plank.area.pill

159 BALTIMORE BEACON

163 LONG STRAND

116 LEACANABUAILE RING FORT

Planning Your Route

Embracing the rugged beauty and untamed spirit of Ireland's western coastline, the Wild Atlantic Way offers an unforgettable journey through a land steeped in history, culture, and breathtaking natural wonders. Spanning over 2,500 kilometres, this astonishing route unveils a treasure trove of enchanting experiences, from the dramatic Cliffs of Moher to the mystical islands of Skellig Michael, each destination whispering tales of ancient lore and timeless beauty.

To truly immerse yourself in the magic of the Wild Atlantic Way, take your time to explore its hidden gems, delve into the vibrant local communities, and savour the sights, sounds, and flavours that define this captivating region. As you traverse the windswept landscapes, you'll find yourself forging deep connections with Ireland's soul-stirring scenery and the warm, welcoming people who call this land home.

While the allure of the Wild Atlantic Way may beckon you to return time and again, it's essential to make the most of each visit by crafting a carefully planned itinerary that showcases the must-see attractions and off-the-beaten-path wonders. Whether it's your first foray into this enchanting realm or a cherished return, the Wild Atlantic Way promises to leave an indelible mark on your heart, kindling a lifelong love affair with the untamed beauty of Ireland's western shores.

7-Day Itinerary on the Wild Atlantic Way

Embark on an unforgettable 7-day adventure along Ireland's Wild Atlantic Way, a 2,500-kilometre coastal route that boasts breathtaking scenery, rich history, and vibrant culture. This itinerary will guide you through a selection of must-see locations, charming towns, and hidden gems along the way.

Day One - Begin your journey in the picturesque town of **Killybegs**, where you can explore the bustling fishing harbour and enjoy a delicious seafood meal. Head west to the majestic **Sliabh Liag Cliffs**, where you'll be rewarded with panoramic views of the Atlantic Ocean. Finish your day in the charming town of **Donegal**, with its traditional Irish pubs and live music.

Day Two - Start your day at the beautiful **Mullaghmore Beach**, perfect for a morning stroll. Continue to the iconic **Benbulben Mountain**, where you can hike the trails or simply admire the stunning landscape. Visit the charming town of **Strandhill**, renowned for its surfing opportunities and seaweed baths. Spend the night in **Sligo** town, exploring its vibrant arts and music scene.

Day Three - Begin with a visit to the impressive **Downpatrick Head**, home to the dramatic sea stack, *Dún Briste*. Next, venture to the **Ceide Fields**, an ancient Neolithic site with fascinating history. Continue to the picturesque town of **Westport**, where you can explore its charming streets and sample local cuisine. Stay overnight in **Westport**, enjoying the lively atmosphere and traditional Irish music.

5 FIVE FINGER STRAND

Day Four - It is time to head south to the vibrant city of **Galway**, where you'll find a thriving arts scene, bustling streets, and colourful shops. This drive will take you through the stunning **Connemara** region, with its rugged landscapes, pristine lakes, and iconic **Twelve Bens** mountain range. Spend the night in the lively and vibrant city of **Galway**, commonly known as one of the best nights out in Ireland.

Day Five - Begin your day at the world-famous **Cliffs of Moher**, where you can walk along the cliff edge and take in the breathtaking views. Continue south through the unique landscape of the **Burren**, a vast limestone plateau rich in geological and archaeological wonders. Arriving on the southern tip of the **Burren Peninsula**, explore the **Kilkee Cliffs** for another perfect example of the dramatic landscape that the west coast has to offer.

Day Six - Travel to the scenic **Dingle Peninsula**, where you can explore the charming town of **Dingle** and its bustling harbour. Drive the stunning **Slea Head Drive**, stopping at the ancient **Gallarus Oratory** and the **Blasket Islands Visitor Centre**. Continue to the picturesque town of **Killarney**, where you can explore the stunning **Killarney National Park**. Stay overnight in **Killarney**, enjoying its vibrant nightlife and traditional Irish hospitality.

Day Seven - Begin your final day with a visit to the colourful town of **Kenmare**, known for its charming streets and artisan shops. Continue to the **Beara Peninsula**, where you can explore the scenic **Healy Pass** and the fascinating **Gairinish Island**. Finish your journey in the bustling city of **Cork**, where you can visit the historic English Market, the impressive St. Fin Barre's Cathedral, and the lively pubs and restaurants.

79 DUNGUAIRE CASTLE

14-Day Itinerary on the Wild Atlantic Way

This two-week adventure allows ample time to explore the stunning landscapes, visit iconic landmarks, and delve into the vibrant local communities that dot the 2,500-kilometre route. With a leisurely pace, you can fully appreciate the breathtaking scenery, engage with the warm Irish hospitality, and create lasting memories, ensuring a well-rounded and unforgettable experience of the Wild Atlantic Way.

Day One - Start your day at the dramatic **Fanad Head Lighthouse**, offering spectacular coastal views out to sea. Then visit the stunning **Marble Bay Strand**, a beautiful beach that is very popular with the locals for swimming, dog-walking, and relaxing. Continue south through **Letterkenny** to the vibrant town of **Donegal** to spend the night amongst its colourful streets and friendly locals.

Day Two - Begin your day in the picturesque town of **Killybegs**, where you can explore the bustling fishing harbour and enjoy a delicious seafood meal. Head west to the majestic **Slaibh Liag Cliffs**, offering panoramic views of the Atlantic Ocean. Visit the stunning **Silver Strand** at Malin Beg, a beautiful and secluded bay on the western coast. Then finish your day in the charming village of **Ardara**, with its traditional Irish pubs and live music.

Day Three - Begin your day at the beautiful **Mullaghmore Beach**, perfect for a morning stroll. Continue to the iconic **Benbulben Mountain**, where you can hike the trails or simply admire the stunning landscape. Visit the charming town of **Strandhill**, renowned for its surfing opportunities and seaweed baths. Spend the night in **Sligo** town, exploring its vibrant arts and music scene.

Day Four - Start with a visit to the impressive **Downpatrick Head**, home to the dramatic sea stack, Dún Briste. Next, venture to the **Ceide Fields**, an ancient Neolithic site with fascinating history. Continue to the picturesque town of **Westport**, where you can explore its charming streets and sample local cuisine. Stay overnight in **Westport**, enjoying the lively atmosphere and traditional Irish music.

Day Five - Travel to the stunning **Achill Island**, connected to the mainland by a bridge. Explore the island's beautiful beaches, such as **Keem Bay** and **Keel Beach**, and visit the dramatic **White Cliffs of Ashleam**. Return to **Westport** for another night of lively Irish entertainment and hospitality.

Day Six - Explore the stunning **Connemara** region, with its rugged landscapes, pristine lakes, and iconic **Twelve Bens** mountain range. Visit the historical **Omey Island**, a religiously significant tidal island that is accessible by foot at low tide. Finally, finish off the day by spending the night in the picturesque town of **Clifden**, with its vibrant atmosphere and historic streets.

Day Seven - Travel south to the vibrant city of **Galway**, where you'll find a thriving arts scene, bustling streets, and colourful shops. Spend the day exploring the city, visiting landmarks such as the **Galway Cathedral**, the **Spanish Arch**, and **Eyre Square**. Enjoy a night out in Galway's lively pubs and restaurants, with live music and traditional Irish dancing.

Day Eight - Visit the beautiful **Aran Islands**, a group of three islands located off the coast of **Galway**. These can be reached direct from Galway City in the summer months, or from **Rossaveal** all year round. Explore the largest island, **Inishmore**, and discover its ancient forts, such as Dún Aonghasa, and beautiful beaches. Return to **Galway** for another night of Irish hospitality.

88 CLIFFS OF MOHER

Day Nine - Begin your day with a visit to the charming village of **Doolin**, renowned for its traditional music and lively atmosphere. Then make your way south to the world-famous **Cliffs of Moher**, where you can walk along the cliff edge and take in the breathtaking views. Explore the unique landscape of the **Burren**, a vast limestone plateau rich in geological and archaeological wonders. Spend the night in the picturesque town of **Ennis**, with its lively pubs and historic streets.

Day Ten - Travel to the historic city of **Limerick**, where you can visit the impressive King John's Castle and the beautiful St. Mary's Cathedral. Explore the city's vibrant arts scene, with its numerous galleries and museums, such as the Hunt Museum. Spend the night in **Limerick**, enjoying its lively pubs and restaurants.

Day Eleven - Travel to the scenic **Dingle Peninsula**, where you can explore the charming town of **Dingle** and its bustling harbour. Drive the stunning **Slea Head Drive**, stopping at the ancient **Gallarus Oratory** and the **Blasket Islands Visitor Centre**. Continue to the picturesque town of **Killarney**, where you can explore the stunning Killarney National Park and Muckross House. Stay overnight in **Killarney**, enjoying its vibrant nightlife and traditional Irish hospitality.

Day Twelve - Embark on a journey around the famous Ring of Kerry, a scenic drive that showcases some of Ireland's most breathtaking landscapes. Visit the picturesque town of **Portmagee**, explore the beautiful beaches at **Ballinskelligs** and **Derrynane**, and peer over the edge of the breathtaking **Kerry Cliffs**. Return to **Killarney** for another night of lively entertainment.

Day Thirteen - Begin your day with a visit to the colourful town of **Kenmare**, known for its charming streets and artisan shops. Continue to the **Beara Peninsula**, where you can explore the scenic **Healy Pass** and the picturesque village of **Eyeries**. Spend the night in the charming coastal town of **Bantry**, with its historic **Bantry House** and beautiful gardens.

Day Fourteen - Finish your journey by driving to the bustling city of **Cork**, cruising along the southern coastline of Ireland. Be sure to stop off along your way at the beautiful beaches, such as **Barley Cove Beach**. If you have time, why not take a trip across to **Cape Clear** and experience the relaxed pace of island life on this southern island. Finally pay a visit to **Cork** and enjoy the busy city streets, toasting to an unforgettable trip before bidding farewell to the Wild Atlantic Way.

137 CASHELKEELTY STONE CIRCLE

One Month Itinerary on the Wild Atlantic Way

The most relaxed and enjoyable length of time to spend exploring the Wild Atlantic Way, 30 days allows you to take your time on the route with days off from the hectic running around of sightseeing. The itinerary for this one-month road trip is the same as the 14-day, with the addition of extra days in County Donegal, County Galway, and some day trips into the picturesque landscapes to enjoy the scenery that the western coast of Ireland has to offer. The sights that we recommend in these extra days are listed below, with the choice of which are best for you being entirely up to yourself.

County Donegal - Begin your adventure in the captivating County Donegal. Visit the stunning stretch of sand at **Carrickfinn Beach** and explore around this isolated part of Ireland. Wander through the charming village of **Glencolmcille**, and explore the ancient stone circles and historic sites. This part of Ireland is chock full of breathtaking beaches, so you will not be disappointed with the choice.

County Sligo - Continue your journey to County Sligo, home to the famous **Benbulben**, a striking table mountain that dominates the landscape. Discover the rich literary heritage of the region, as it inspired the works of poet W.B. Yeats. Visit the charming coastal town of **Strandhill** and enjoy a rejuvenating seaweed bath or take a stroll along the sandy beach.

County Mayo - In County Mayo, explore the breathtaking landscapes of **Achill Island**, Ireland's largest island, as well as the underrated **Mullet Peninsula** to its north. Discover the stunning **Keem Bay**, a secluded beach surrounded by dramatic cliffs, and hike the **Croaghaun Mountain** for panoramic views.

County Galway - Explore Country Galway's allure beyond the Connemara National Park and Galway city. Discover the enchanting **Kylemore Abbey**, nestled by a serene lake, the intriguing Connemara Smokehouse, where the finest smoked salmon is crafted, and the picturesque village of **Clifden**, famed for its vibrant atmosphere and captivating shops. You can then finish off the day with a stunning sunset at the **Sky Road Lookout**.

County Clare - County Clare is home to the iconic **Cliffs of Moher**, a must-visit attraction along the Wild Atlantic Way, however there is also so much more to it than that. All along the western coast of this region, the dramatic cliffs can be found towering out of the ocean. Head further south from Moher to the **Kilkee Cliffs** and the **Bridges of Ross** for a more tranquil area to enjoy the majesty of the Atlantic Ocean.

County Kerry - Journey to the enchanting County Kerry, home to the famous **Ring of Kerry**, a scenic drive that showcases the region's awe-inspiring beauty. The most underappreciated sights in this area lie on the far western coast of the route, as

74 DOG'S BAY

well as on the peninsula to the south of it. Spend some time exploring the far west of the Kerry Peninsula, such as Valentia Island, and the pass across to **St Finan's Bay**, for a truly unique side to the route. Then head south onto the **Beara Peninsula** and drive the winding roads around its western edge. This part of Ireland is the closest we have found anywhere on earth to the beauty of the Wester Ross region of Scotland.

County Cork - Conclude your Wild Atlantic Way adventure in the captivating County Cork. Explore the bustling city of Cork, known for its lively food and music scene. Visit the historic **Blarney Castle** and kiss the famous Blarney Stone to receive the gift of eloquence. Discover the picturesque fishing villages of **Kinsale** and **Cobh**, where you can indulge in delicious seafood and soak up the charming atmosphere.

154 MIZEN HEAD

Index

Sights

Aasleigh Falls	148
Abbey Island	224
Achill-Henge	133
Allihies Copper Mine	241
Altar Wedge Tomb	254
Annagh Head	128
Ashleam Bay	132
Aughadown Graveyard	257
Ballaghasheen Pass View	227
Ballinskelligs Bay	223
Ballybunion	190
Ballycrovane Ogham Stone	239
Ballydonegan Beach	242
Ballyheigue Beach	190
Ballyhiernan Beach	73
Ballymastocker Beach	72
Ballyvaughan	176
Baltimore Beacon	257
Bantry House	245
Barleycove	254
Benbulbin	103
Benwee Head	118
Blasket Centre	204
Blennerville Windmill	191
Bloody Foreland	76
Brandon Point	201
Bridges of Ross	188
Bromore Cliffs	190
Bunbeg	77
Burren	175
Caha Pass	237
Cape Clear	256
Caragh Lake	217
Carrickabraghy Castle	57
Carrickfin Beach	77
Carrigafoyle Castle	189
Carrigaholt	188
Carrowmore Beach	115
Cashelkeelty Stone Circle	238
Castlegregory Beach	201
Castletown-Bearhaven	244
Ceide Fields	117
Charles Fort	264
Claggan Island	129
Cleggan Harbour	150
Clifden Castle	152
Cliffs of Moher	177
Cloonee Lough	236
Cnoc Droma Stone Fort	258
Cobh	264
Connemara National park	162
Coppingers Court	265
Corcomroe Abbey	174
Cork	265
Coumeenole Beach	207
Courtmacsherry	263
Croagh Patrick	146
Crohy Head	89
Crookhaven	255
Derreen Garden	237
Derry Walls	62
Derrynane Beach	224
Dingle	208
Doe Castle	75
Dog's Bay	162
Donegal	92
Dooks Beach	218
Doolough Valley Memorial	147
Dooneen Pier	202
Downpatrick Head	117
Drombeg Stone Circle	260
Dugort Beach	134
Dunbeg Fort	208
Dunboy Castle	244
Dunguaire Castle	173
Dunquin	204
Dunree Head	61
Dursey Sound	243
Elly bay Beach	128
Fanad Head Lighthouse	73
Fanore Beach	176
Fermoyle Strand	201
Five Finger Strand	54
Flaggy Shore	175
Fogher Cliffs (Aillte Fogher)	220
Gallarus Oratory	202
Gap of Dunloe	227
Gap of Mamore	59
Garinish Beach	242
Glanageenty Forest	191
Glanmore Lake	238
Glencar Waterfall	105
Glenevin Waterfall	59
Glengarriff	245
Great Pollet Sea Arch	72
Healy Pass Waterfall & Tunnel	238
Hungry Hill	245
Inch Island	62
Inchydoney Beach	260
Inis Cathaigh	188
Inishbiggle	129
Inisheer	177
Inishmore	177
Isle of Doagh	56
Keem Strand	133
Kerry Cliffs (Aillte Chiarraí)	221
Kilcatherine Church	239
Kilclooney	90
Kildavnet Tower	136
Kilkee Cliffs	188
Kinnagoe Bay	52
Kinny Lough	73
Kylemore Abbey	149
Lahinch	177
Leacanabuaile Ring Fort	218
Lisfannon Beach	61
Loher Stone Fort	223
Long Strand	260
Maghera Beach	91
Malin Head	53
Marble Hill Strand	75
Minard Castle	209
Mizen Head	255
Moll's Gap	226
Mount Gabriel	256
Moyteoge Head	134
Muckinish West Tower House	175
Mullaghmore Head	106
Mulranny Beach	136
Murder Hole Beach	73
Murvagh Beach	101
Mutton Island	165
Old Head Beach	147
Old Head of Kinsale	264
Omey Island	150
Pollan Strand	58
Portmagee	221
Puffin Island	221
Pulleen Harbour	243
Raghly	103
Ramelton	72
Renvyle Beach	149
Rockfleet Castle	134
Rosserk Friary	115
Roundstone	164
Shannon Estuary	189
Sherkin Island	258
Silver Strand	148
Silverstrand Beach	165
Slea Head	207
Sliabh Liag	92
Sligo Abbey	105
Smerwich Harbour	204
Spiddal Pier	164
Staigue Stone Fort	226
Stroove beach	52
The Hag of Beara	241
The Lost Valley	148
Valentia Island Footprints	219
Timoleague Friary	263
Tory island	76
Tranarossan Bay	75
Trawbreaga Bay	54

Tullagh Bay	58	
Tullan Strand (Fairy Bridge)	102	
Uragh Stone Circle	235	
Valentia Island Lighthouse	219	
Vaughan's Pass	245	
White Cliffs of Ashleam	131	
Wild Nephin National Park	129	
Woodland Faerie Trail	132	

Accommodation

1 Closheen Lane, Ross Carbery	267
18 Ard na Mara, Dingle	211
20 Lighthouse Village	193
25 Millers Way	64
6 Gortonora	211
Achill Seal Caves Campsite	138
Actons Hotel Kinsale	267
All the Twos Guesthouse	154
Allihies Holiday Homes	247
An Riasc Farmhouse Rental	211
Anchor Caravan Park	211
Ardagh Hotel & Restaurant	167
Ardmore Country House	154
Armada Hotel	193
Arranmore Glamping	94
Art House	64
Asgard Apartments	154
Atlantic Caravan Park	120
Avondale House	138
Ballynahinch Castle	167
Barleycove Holiday Park	267
Barr na Sraide Inn	211
Base Accommodation Dingle	211
Beara Camping	247
Beara Coast Hotel	247
Beara Holiday Homes	247
Beechwood, Londonderry	64
Belleek Park Campsite	120
Ben Lettery Hostel	167
Berehaven Lodge	247
Berehaven Pods	247
Binion Bay Campsite	64
Bishop's Gate Hotel Derry	64
Boortree Touring	108
Bunbeg Lodge	82
Campail Teach an Aragail	211
Casey's Hotel, Glengarriff	247
Caseys Caravan & Camping	82
Cashel House Hotel	167
Castle Grove Country House	82
Castle View Rooms	181
Cavangarden Court	108
Ceann Sibeal Hotel	211
Ceide Glamping	120
Celtic Ross Hotel	267
Clew Bay Cottage	138
Clifden Eco Beach	154
Cliffs Of Moher Hotel	181
Connemara Camping	154
Coolmore Manor House	108
Corcreggan Mill	82
Corr an Droma	267
Corrakille House	94
Crag Na Cor B&B	64
Creevy Pier Hotel	108
Cute Coastal Village Retreat	267
Delphi Lodge	154
Delphi Resort	154
Devlin Farm Life	154
Dingle Bay Hotel	211
Dingle Benners Hotel	211
Dingle Marina Cottages	211
Dingle Skellig Hotel	211
Doolough Dream	138
Drumbarron Cottage	94
Dunaras Self Catering	167
Dungloe Caravan Park	94
Dungloe Rooms	94
Dunowen House, Clonakilty	267
Eccles Hotel and Spa	247
Emlaghmore Cottage	167
Eyeries MotorHome Park	247
Fallons Bed & Breakfast	181
Fanore Self Catering	181
Fleming's White Bridge	229
Foyleside Caravan Park	64
Further Space at Belmullet	138
Galway Coast Cottages	167
Geraghtys Farmyard Pods	138
Gleesk Pier Cottage	229
Glenbeg Caravan & Camping	229
Glór na hAbhann, Dingle	211
Gortnor Abbey Pier Aire	120
Green Acres Caravan Park	211
Greenlands Caravan & Camping	108
Greystone House	138
Half Acre Cottage	167
Hazelbrook Farmhouse B&B	154
Heron's Cove	108
Heyday Ballina	120
Holland House B&B	108
Hungry Hill Campsite	247
Hylands Burren Hotel	181
Ice House Hotel	120
Into The Burren	181
Jacks Country Farmhouse	211
Keel Camping	138
Kilcommon Lodge Hostel	120
Killala Holiday Village	120
Kinhart's Moy Estuary House	120
Klondell House	193
Klondell House Lahinch	181
Knockbroughaun Cottage	167
Lahinch Coast Hotel	181
Lahinch Coast Hotel	193
Lakeside Caravan & Camping	108
Lakeside House Killarney	229
Lavelle's Seaside House	138
Lavelles Seaside House	138
Leam Cottage	138
Lehinch Lodge	193
Lissadell Holiday Apartment	64
M033 Achill Gatehouse	138
Malinbeg Hostel	94
Mannix Point Campsite	229
Menlo Park Self Catering	167
Milltown House Dingle	211
Mount Errigal Hotel	82
Mulroy Woods Hotel	82
Murlach Lodge	167
Murrayville B&B	138
Murrisk Apartments	154
Nagles Camping & Caravan	181
Nevins Motorhome Park	138
O'Connor's Riverside Park	181
O'Connors Guesthouse	211
Ocean View Park	193
Once Upon a Tide	154
Park Hotel Kenmare	229
Park Hotel Kenmare	247
Parknasilla Resort and Spa	229
Quiet Moments Camping	82
Rays Country Cottages	181
Red Deer Cottage	154
Redcastle Hotel	64
Renvyle 353 Lake Cottage	154
Renvyle Beach Campsite	154
Ridgepool View	120
Rock Cottage Country House	267
Rosebank Apartments	64
Rossmore Farmhouse B&B	108
Rossnowlagh Waves Lodge	108
RUA Camping Inis Oírr	181
Rugged Glen	247
Salthill Caravan Camping	167
Schull Harbour Hotel	267
Sea Stack View	120
Seacoast Lodge	181
Seal Cottage	247
Sextons Caravan & Camping	267
Shamrock Inn Hotel	193
Shandon Hotel & Spa	82
Shannon Springs Hotel	193
Sheen Falls Lodge	229

Silver Birch House	229
Sleepy Hollows	82
Sleepzone Galway Hostel	167
Sliabh Liag Camping	94
Slieve League Inn	94
Song House	82
Spiddal Caravan & Camping	167
Strand Camping	193
Sunset Lodge	108
Surfers Delight Home	108
Tara Hotel	94
Teach Cruachan B&B	138
The Abbey Hotel	94
The Acres Killala	120
The Ashe Hotel	193
The Barleycove Beach Hotel	267
The Courtyard Apartments	193
The Dingle Galley	211
The Dunloe Hotel	229
The Europe Hotel & Resort	229
The Grand Hotel	193
The Grove Cottage	229
The Hideaway Campsite	267
The Honeycomb Chalet	108
The Imperial Hotel & Spa	267
The Killarney Park	229
The Lodge at Friars Glen	229
The Lodge Doolin	181
The Lodges @ Sea View	181
The Loft	94
The Merry Monk	120
The Old Deanery Cottages	120
The Sandhouse Hotel	108
The Sleepy Leprechaun	181
The Snug Townhouse	167
The Waterfoot Hotel	64
The Waterfront Hotel	267
The Waters Country House	181
The Western Strands	138
The Willows	193
Tir na Hilan Self Catering	247
Tramore Beach Campsite	94
Trident Holiday Homes	94
Waterfront Hotel	94
Westport Coast Hotel	154
Wild Atlantic Hostel	154
Woodhill House	94
Woodlands Park	193
Woodview, Ennis	193

Dining

Anthony's at Doolin Inn	180
Batch Donegal	81
Bellbridge House Hotel	192
Blueberry Tea Room	93
Breen's Lobster Bar	246
Caffe Banbha Malin Head	63
Casey's Bar and Restaurant	246
Casey's of Baltimore	266
Chill the Beans	93
Claire the Bakers	63
Coach Lane - Donaghy's Bar	107
Crêpe Hatch	81
Cronin's Sheebeen	153
Crotty's Pub and B&B	192
Dillons Bar & Restaurant	119
Eithna's By the Sea	107
Finnegans	166
Fisk Seafood Bar Downings	81
Flipside	107
Gilroy's Bar and Áit Eile	119
Greenes Restaurant	266
Hazel Mountain Chocolate	180
Helen's Bar	246
Henrys Bar & Restaurant	107
Keane's Bar & Restaurant	192
Leo's Tavern	81
Little Fish Cafe, Cleggan	153
Louisburgh 74 - Café Bistro	153
Lowry's Bar	153
Mary's Bakery	119
Mc's Bistro & Grill	137
McGrory's Hotel Culdaff	63
Mitchell's Restaurant	153
Monks Ballyvaughan	180
Murphy's Restaurant	246
Nephin Restaurant	137
Nevin's Newfield Inn	137
No. 35	246
O'Carroll's Cove	228
Out of the Blue Seafood	210
Owenmore Restaurant	166
Pisces Restaurant	210
Poacher Restaurant	119
Quinn's Pub: The Ventry Inn	210
Rambling House	107
Raviolo Verde	180
Royal Garden Chinese	166
Salthill Cabin	93
Scannells Bar	266
Scarpello & Co	63
Scarriff Inn Restaurant	228
Shannon's Corner Restaurant	107
Signal Bar and Restaurant	166
Sizzlers Restaurant	119
Skelligs Chocolate and Cafe	228
Solas Tapas & Wine Bar	210
Stone Barn Cafe	137
Sugarloaf Cafe	246
The Blind Piper	228
The Bulman Bar & Restaurant	266
The Chart House	210
The Cross, Achill Island	137
The Currach	137
The Fish Box	210
The Fish Kitchen	266
The Glandore Inn	266
The Harbour Restaurant	93
The Hungry Veggie	180
The Larder, Ballyvaughan	180
The Lobster Bar & Restaurant	228
The Lobster Pot	93
The Long Dock	192
The Old Post Office	119
The Oratory	228
The Pantry	192
The Quays Bar and Restaurant	166
The Quilty Tavern	192
The Railway Tavern	63
The Rusty Mackerel	93
The Rusty Nail	63
The Rusty Oven - Pizzeria	81
The Shack	81
The Towers Bar & Restaurant	153
Tigh Mheaic	166

Written:
Gemma Spence
Campbell Kerr

Photos:
Gemma Spence
Campbell Kerr

Editing:
Gemma Spence
Campbell Kerr
Natasha Gooch (NG Remote VA)
Shiva Shahriari (iOB Design)

Design:
Campbell Kerr
Shiva Shahriari (iOB Design)
Gary Fu (Rocktiger Designs)

Scan the barcode below for access to the Destination Atlantic Way map, showing all sights listed in this book

Photo copyrights:
Copyright © 2023 Campbell Kerr, Gemma Spence. All rights reserved. The moral rights of the authors have been asserted. All photos © 2023 Gemma Spence and Campbell Kerr.

Author Acknowledgements:
The support of our family and friends, as well as those who support us online does not go unnoticed and we want to send a heartfelt thanks to all of you. Our motorhome Ellie has also brought us on all of these crazy adventures and without her, we really would not be able to spend as much time as we do researching each destination inside and out. We also want to extend a huge thank you to Gary and Shiva for their creative and design skills throughout the book and Tash for her support in compiling information. The hard work of all involved does not go unnoticed.

Health, Safety, and Responsibility:
As with any outdoor and adventure activity, from land to water-based, there is always a level of risk with those discussed in this book. The locations in this book are all prone to dangerous conditions caused by nature, floods, droughts, high winds, severe rain, snow, and foggy conditions. While the authors of this book have gone to great lengths to ensure the accuracy of the information provided in this book, they will not be held legally or financially responsible for any accident, injury, loss or inconvenience sustained as a result of the information or advice contained in this guide. All activities that are discussed in this book are done entirely at the reader's own risk.

LIKE ANY PICTURES? GET A CANVAS PRINT
All pictures shown in this guide, as well as many others that were captured along the route, are all available for canvas print for you to enjoy in your home. Visit our website shown below for the full range of prints, or get in touch at the email below for any special requests.

Get in touch - **contact@destinationearthguides.com**

www.destinationearthguides.com